T5-BQA-587

DATE

An Approach to Federal Urban Policy

A Statement on National Policy
by the Research and Policy Committee
of the Committee for Economic Development

December 1977

DISCARD

Andrew S. Thomas Memorial Library
MORRIS HARVEY COLLEGE, CHARLESTON, W. VA.

96464

30926
C737a

Library of Congress Cataloging in Publication Data

Committee for Economic Development.
  An approach to Federal urban policy.

  Includes bibliographical references.
  1. Cities and towns—United States.   2. Federal-city
relations—United States.   I. Title.
HT123.C613   1977   309.2'62'0973   77-27893
ISBN 0-87186-065-1

First printing: December 1977
Paperbound: $2.50
Library binding: $4.00
Printed in the United States of America by Dunshaw Press
Design: John Marshall

COMMITTEE FOR ECONOMIC DEVELOPMENT
477 Madison Avenue, New York, N.Y. 10022
1700 K Street, N.W., Washington, D.C. 20006

Contents

Responsibility for CED Statements on National Policy

The Committee for Economic Development is an independent research and educational organization of two hundred business executives and educators. CED is nonprofit, nonpartisan, and nonpolitical. Its purpose is to propose policies that will help to bring about steady economic growth at high employment and reasonably stable prices, increase productivity and living standards, provide greater and more equal opportunity for every citizen, and improve the quality of life for all. A more complete description of the objectives and organization of CED is to be found on page 48.

All CED policy recommendations must have the approval of the Research and Policy Committee, a group of trustees whose names are listed on these pages. This Committee is directed under the bylaws to "initiate studies into the principles of business policy and of public policy which will foster the full contribution by industry and commerce to the attainment and maintenance" of the objectives stated above. The bylaws emphasize that "all research is to be thoroughly objective in character, and the approach in each instance is to be from the standpoint of the general welfare and not from that of any special political or economic group." The Committee is aided by a Research Advisory Board of leading social scientists and by a small permanent professional staff.

Research and Policy Committee

Chairman: FRANKLIN A. LINDSAY
Vice Chairmen: JOHN L. BURNS / *Education and Social and Urban Development*
E. B. FITZGERALD / *International Economy*
HOWARD C. PETERSEN / *National Economy*
WAYNE E. THOMPSON / *Improvement of Management in Government*

[1] A. ROBERT ABBOUD	ROBERT J. CARLSON	FRANCIS E. FERGUSON
SANFORD S. ATWOOD	[3] RAFAEL CARRION, JR.	JOHN H. FILER
JOSEPH W. BARR	WILLIAM S. CASHEL, JR.	E. B. FITZGERALD
HARRY HOOD BASSETT	JOHN B. CAVE	JOHN M. FOX
JACK F. BENNETT	EMILIO G. COLLADO	DAVID L. FRANCIS
CHARLES P. BOWEN, JR.	ROBERT C. COSGROVE	WILLIAM H. FRANKLIN
JOHN L. BURNS	JOHN H. DANIELS	JOHN D. GRAY
[1] FLETCHER L. BYROM	W. D. EBERLE	TERRANCE HANOLD

4

The Research and Policy Committee is not attempting to pass judgment on any pending specific legislative proposals; its purpose is to urge careful consideration of the objectives set forth in this statement and of the best means of accomplishing those objectives.

Each statement on national policy is preceded by discussions, meetings, and exchanges of memoranda, often stretching over many months. The research is undertaken by a subcommittee, assisted by advisors chosen for their competence in the field under study. The members and advisors of the subcommittee that prepared this statement are listed on page 6.

The full Research and Policy Committee participates in the drafting of findings and recommendations. Likewise, the trustees on the drafting subcommittee vote to approve or disapprove a policy statement, and they share with the Research and Policy Committee the privilege of submitting individual comments for publication, as noted on this and the following page and on the appropriate page of the text of the statement.

Except for the members of the Research and Policy Committee and the responsible subcommittee, the recommendations presented herein are not necessarily endorsed by other trustees or by the advisors, contributors, staff members, or others associated with CED.

H. J. HEINZ, II	GEORGE C. McGHEE	[1] ROBERT B. SEMPLE
ROBERT C. HOLLAND	E. L. McNEELY	ROCCO C. SICILIANO
GILBERT E. JONES	[1] J. W. McSWINEY	ROGER B. SMITH
EDWARD R. KANE	[1] ROBERT R. NATHAN	CHARLES B. STAUFFACHER
[1] CHARLES KELLER, JR.	HOWARD C. PETERSEN	WILLIAM C. STOLK
JAMES R. KENNEDY	[1] C. WREDE PETERSMEYER	WALTER N. THAYER
PHILIP M. KLUTZNICK	R. STEWART RAUCH, JR.	WAYNE E. THOMPSON
RALPH LAZARUS	[1] JAMES Q. RIORDAN	J. W. VAN GORKOM
FRANKLIN A. LINDSAY	MELVIN J. ROBERTS	SIDNEY J. WEINBERG, JR.
G. BARRON MALLORY	WILLIAM M. ROTH	GEORGE L. WILCOX
THOMAS B. McCABE	HENRY B. SCHACHT	[2] FRAZAR B. WILDE

[1] Voted to approve the policy statement but submitted memoranda of comment, reservation, or dissent or wished to be associated with memoranda of others. See pages 34–37.
[2] Voted to disapprove this statement.
[3] Did not participate in the voting on this statement because of absence from the country.
NOTE/A complete list of CED trustees and honorary trustees appears at the back of the book. *Company or institutional associations are included for identification only; the organizations do not share in the responsibility borne by the individuals.*

Subcommittee on Revitalizing America's Cities

Chairman
PHILIP M. KLUTZNICK
Klutznick Investments

[1] A. ROBERT ABBOUD, Chairman
The First National Bank of Chicago

JAMES F. BERÉ, Chairman
Borg-Warner Corporation

[1] R. MANNING BROWN, JR., Chairman
New York Life Insurance Co., Inc.

JOHN L. BURNS, President
John L. Burns and Company

RONALD R. DAVENPORT, Chairman
Sheridan Broadcasting Corporation

[1] ROBERT R. DOCKSON, Chairman
California Federal Savings and
  Loan Association

WILLIAM S. EDGERLY
Chairman and President
State Street Bank and Trust Company

JOHN T. FEY, Chairman
The Equitable Life Assurance
  Society of the United States

JOHN H. FILER, Chairman
Aetna Life and Casualty Company

HUGH M. GLOSTER, President
Morehouse College

[1] JOHN D. GRAY, Chairman
Hart Schaffner & Marx

JOHN D. GRAY, Chairman
Omark Industries, Inc.

SAMUEL C. JOHNSON, Chairman
S. C. Johnson & Son, Inc.

[1] CHARLES KELLER, JR.,
New Orleans, Louisiana

CHARLES N. KIMBALL, Chairman
Midwest Research Institute

HARRY W. KNIGHT, Chairman
Hillsboro Associates, Inc.

RALPH LAZARUS, Chairman
Federated Department Stores, Inc.

DONALD S. MacNAUGHTON
Chairman
Prudential Insurance Company of
  America

JEAN MAYER, President
Tufts University

CHAMPNEY A. McNAIR, Vice Chairman
Trust Company of Georgia

CHAUNCEY J. MEDBERRY, III
Chairman
Bank of America N.T. & S.A.

CHARLES A. MEYER,
Vice President and Director
Sears, Roebuck and Company

[1] ROBERT R. NATHAN, President
Robert R. Nathan Associates, Inc.

VICTOR H. PALMIERI, President
Victor Palmieri and Company Incorporated

[1] JOHN H. PERKINS, President
Continental Illinois National Bank
  and Trust Company of Chicago

PETER G. PETERSON, Chairman
Lehman Brothers, Inc.

DONALD C. PLATTEN, Chairman
Chemical Bank

R. STEWART RAUCH, JR., Chairman
The Philadelphia Saving Fund Society

MELVIN J. ROBERTS
Colorado National Bankshares, Inc.

RICHARD B. SELLARS
Chairman, Finance Committee
Johnson & Johnson

RICHARD R. SHINN, President
Metropolitan Life Insurance Company

ROCCO C. SICILIANO, Chairman
TICOR

WILLIS A. STRAUSS, Chairman
Northern Natural Gas Company

HOWARD S. TURNER, Chairman
Turner Construction Company

[2] ROBERT C. WEAVER
Department of Urban Affairs
Hunter College

WILLIAM H. WENDEL, President
The Carborundum Company

[2] FRAZAR B. WILDE, Chairman Emeritus
Connecticut General Life Insurance
  Company

J. KELLEY WILLIAMS, President
First Mississippi Corporation

MARGARET S. WILSON, Chairman
Scarbroughs

Ex Officio

WILLIAM H. FRANKLIN

ROBERT C. HOLLAND

FRANKLIN A. LINDSAY

WAYNE E. THOMPSON

Nontrustee members

NORMAN E. AUERBACH, Chairman
Coopers & Lybrand

CARLA A. HILLS
Washington, D.C.

FELIX G. ROHATYN, General Partner
Lazard Freres & Company

[1] Voted to approve the policy statement but submitted memoranda of comment, reservation, or dissent or
wished to be associated with memoranda of others.
[2] Voted to disapprove this statement.
*Nontrustee members take part in all discussions on the statement but do not vote on it.

Advisors to the Subcommittee

ROY BAHL
Professor of Economics
The Maxwell School of Citizenship
  and Public Affairs
Syracuse University

ANTHONY DOWNS
The Brookings Institution

LYLE C. FITCH, President
Institute of Public Administration

LEWIS HILL
Commissioner of Department of
  Development and Planning
City of Chicago

HARVEY PERLOFF
Professor of Architecture
  and Urban Affairs
University of California

WILLIAM L. RAFSKY, President
Center for Philadelphia Area
  Development

Co-Project Directors

R. SCOTT FOSLER
Director, Government Studies
Committee for Economic Development

HARVEY A. GARN
Program Director of Urban Development,
  Processes and Indicator Research
The Urban Institute

Project Editor

CLAUDIA P. FEUREY
Associate Director of Information
Committee for Economic Development

6

Foreword

Purpose of This Statement

The CED Research and Policy Committee has long been concerned with the health and character of the nation's cities. In recent years, the Committee has published a number of statements on issues central to city life — improving health care, education, and housing; reforming the welfare system; and restructuring urban government.

The CED Subcommittee on Revitalizing America's Cities continues the work of identifying the major forces that are affecting this country's urban areas and developing recommendations about why and how public policies should respond to these forces. This introductory report, *An Approach to Federal Urban Policy,* was prepared against the background of an intensifying debate over a national urban policy. As a contribution to the public discussion, the subcommittee felt it was important to make a brief initial statement about the general direction federal urban policy should take.

This statement is timely and significant for several reasons. First, it stresses the often neglected fact that different cities have different problems; and it outlines ways in which the federal government can take these many differences into account. Second, it proposes a set of key elements that are essential to develop the mechanisms and sustained leadership necessary to deal with the problems of the cities. It calls particularly on private industry, state and local governments, and citizens to explore new means of identifying and implementing solutions to urban life.

We wish to emphasize, however, that this is an introductory statement. The Subcommittee on Revitalizing America's Cities is moving forward with a more comprehensive and detailed examination of how urban programs should be tailored to the diverse and complex needs of urban areas.

This report was prepared under the chairmanship of Philip M. Klutznick, former chairman of Urban Investment and Development Company in Chicago. Mr. Klutznick's knowledge and experience in urban affairs and his deep commitment to urban life in this country make him exemplary among the nation's business leaders. Mr. Klutznick will continue to direct future reports issued by this subcommittee.

The members of the subcommittee, listed on page 6, represent a wide range of extraordinary talents and abilities from the fields of business, education, and government. We are especially indebted to Mr. Klutznick, to the members of this subcommittee, and to the fresh and constructive approach of co-project directors Harvey A. Garn, Program Director of Urban Development, Processes, and Indicator Research, The Urban Institute, and R. Scott Fosler, Director, Government Studies, Committee for Economic Development.

Franklin A. Lindsay, *Chairman*
Research and Policy Committee

SUMMARY AND RECOMMENDATIONS

Achieving healthy economic development in urban areas is a vital factor in achieving the healthy growth of the total economy.

There is no single urban problem. Rather, the economic and social problems of urban areas vary considerably. Consequently, there is no single or simple solution to the nation's urban problems. Improvements in urban areas require different approaches for different problems.

Private industry, state and local governments, and citizen groups must all participate in solving urban problems. The federal government must supplement local efforts both because of the impact of current federal policies on urban areas and because many of the problems that face the cities exceed the local capacity to solve them.

In subsequent policy statements, CED's Subcommittee on Revitalizing America's Cities will analyze a broad range of urban problems and offer recommendations for remedies to them.* Whereas this introductory statement concentrates on federal policy considerations, a major part of the forthcoming study will focus on what local government, business, and community groups can do. That focus reflects CED's belief that all these groups have a responsibility to participate in the development of successful urban strategies for the present and the future.

The present Administration has set as one of its goals the development of policies to help deal with the problems of America's cities. It further seeks to develop and support the leadership necessary to sustain this effort. We recognize the importance and complexity of this undertaking. We also recognize that there is not, nor can there be, any once-and-for-all solution to urban problems. Nevertheless, some key elements of a federal urban strategy can be recommended. We believe that these recommendations can do much to help focus the federal government's effort to improve its response to urban problems.**

Systematic monitoring of the effects of federal policies on the distribution of the labor force and economic activity is essential.

The federal government should assume responsibility for direct income transfers to the poor.***

*See memorandum by JOHN D. GRAY, page 34.

**See memorandum by FRAZAR B. WILDE, page 34.

***See memoranda by FLETCHER L. BYROM, and by JOHN H. PERKINS, pages 34 and 35.

Federal policy must be sharply focused on economic development programs directly related to particular cities' problems and on new mechanisms for ensuring effective federal participation.

Because one set of strategies will not achieve economic development objectives in all places, the federal government must develop procedures for identifying priorities among places to be served and for providing assistance to those programs that best meet the needs of those particular places.

The federal government should encourage—at the very least it should not frustrate—both active efforts and developing potential of local leadership to bring together public and private resources for the productive resolution of the problems of the cities.

We believe that the time has come for federal policy to recognize the diversity of local areas, to be prepared to respond to local needs, and to make use of all that can be learned at the local level about how improvements can be made. The federal government needs an approach that is both more flexible than categorical grants and more focused on specific plans than general revenue sharing. It must make a commitment to well-planned improvements in the nation's central cities.

INTRODUCTION

The health of the nation's cities is a vital factor in determining the nation's economic health. This Committee has recognized the close relationship between healthy cities and the strength and stability of the U.S. economy, calling attention to it in a series of policy statements issued since 1960. Many cities have long faced severe economic and social problems, and in recent years, these problems have worsened. Such cities are marked by an erosion of human and physical resources, widening economic disparities and inequities, and growing problems of race and poverty.

This Committee is dedicated to the goals of achieving high employment, price stability, increased productivity, and greater opportunity for all Americans. A critical element in reaching these goals is more successful resolution of the nation's urban dilemmas.

Local private initiative and effective participation by local governments are indispensable to that successful resolution. The federal government can help through well-designed programs aimed at promoting a healthy urban society, and recent signs of a growing federal commitment to revitalizing America's cities are encouraging and most welcome. The time has come for the federal, state, and city governments to forge a creative new partnership with private enterprise to combat urban problems.

The purpose of this introductory statement is twofold: It highlights some critical differences among urban areas, and it points the way to developing constructive federal approaches that will take such differences into account. It goes on to trace some of the implications of making the healthy development of urban areas a central element of federal policy.

Many key questions remain unanswered. Exactly how urban programs should be tailored to meet the diverse and complex needs of America's cities is the subject of continuing study and debate. CED's Subcommittee on Revitalizing America's Cities, which prepared this introductory statement, is engaged in an intensive examination of these issues. More comprehensive studies will be forthcoming in the course of the Subcommittee's work.

This statement is based on five fundamental propositions:

- Achieving healthy economic development in urban areas is a vital part of achieving the healthy growth of the national economy.

- There is no single urban problem. The economic and social problems of urban areas vary considerably.

- There is no single or simple solution to the nation's urban problems. Different approaches are required to deal with different problems and bring about significant improvements.

- State and local governments, private industry, and citizen groups must play major roles in identifying and implementing appropriate solutions to urban problems.

- The federal government must supplement local efforts both because of the impact of current federal policies on urban areas and because many urban problems exceed the capacity of individual areas to solve them.

We emphasize that healthy economic development of an urban area does not require any particular population level or job level. Adjustments in both may be necessary to achieve a sustainable balance of the two.

TRENDS IN POPULATION AND ECONOMIC ACTIVITY

Any strategy to cope with urban economic and social problems must take into account the changes in location of population and economic activity that are occurring in the United States. The two major relevant trends are shifts of population and economic activity from one region to another and decentralization of population and economic activity within metropolitan areas throughout the nation.[1]

The main feature of the regional shifts has been the relatively slow growth rates in the Northeast and North Central regions compared with the higher growth rates in the West and South. Between 1960 and 1970, the population of the Northeast and North Central regions grew by 9.8 percent and 9.6 percent, respectively; during the same period, the West grew by 24.1 percent and the South by 14.2 percent. This trend has accelerated since 1970. From 1970 to 1975, population grew by only 0.9 percent in the Northeast and 1.9 percent in the North Central region. The West grew by 8.8 percent and the South by 8.5 percent during the same period. Regional shifts in employment have roughly paralleled this pattern. In 1949, the Northeast and North Central regions provided jobs for over 62 percent of the nation's nonagricultural employees. Now, they provide only slightly more than 50 percent of such jobs. Current evidence does not suggest any imminent reversal of these regional trends.

Decentralization of population and businesses from traditional central-city jurisdictions is another pronounced trend. Population is even more widely dispersed than jobs within metropolitan areas. However, since 1948, the rate of *job dispersal* has been higher than the rate of *population dispersal*, reflecting the fact that the economic base of a metropolitan area extends well beyond the central city. All major categories of employment (manufacturing, retailing, services, and wholesaling) have dispersed rapidly and are now spread nearly as widely as population. (Recent data on employment changes are provided in Figure 1 of the Appendix.)

As in the case of the regional trends, there is no evidence that continued decentralization of population and economic activity will soon be reversed. In fact, the most recent evidence shows decentralization spreading beyond current metropolitan boundaries and increasing the

1. For an excellent discussion of these general trends, their implications for urban problems, and possible solutions, see William Gorham and Nathan Glazer, eds., *The Urban Predicament* (Washington, D.C.: The Urban Institute, 1976).

14

nonmetropolitan population as well (see Appendix, Figure 3). Between 1970 and 1975, many metropolitan areas lost population to their suburban and rural fringes. From March 1975 to March 1976, about 400,000 more people moved out of metropolitan areas than moved into them from nonmetropolitan areas.[2] However, this does not mean that there is a major reorientation toward rural living. Rather, many of the nonmetropolitan areas experiencing population increases are within commuting distance of metropolitan areas.

The reasons for these two major shifts in population and economic activity are many and varied. However, certain key causes are prevalent in enough cities to deserve special mention. First is the high cost of working or operating a business in a center city, particularly in some congested cities in the Northeast. Second is a relative decline in the quality of city life, which is reflected in higher crime rates, poor educational systems, and deteriorating cultural and recreational opportunities. Sometimes, changes of location are prompted by the combination of declining conditions and more attractive alternatives in the suburbs or in another part of the country. CED has studied some of these particular urban problems in the past and will give them further attention in its future study of the cities. Given current policies, these forces may continue to encourage the movement of population and employment away from center cities and to their suburbs or to other regions.

These two trends indicate that few cities or metropolitan areas can expect to have stable levels of population and employment. Some will grow; others will lose population and employment. To a large degree, such changes are necessary and effective adaptations to new circumstances. However, not all changes are so benign as that general observation implies. Furthermore, the generalization does not apply equally to all urban areas. The issue is much more complex.

Many of the most severe problems resulting from these trends appear to be concentrated in cities that are losing population. However, in some of these areas, population decline is not accompanied by substantial job loss. Such cities may retain their vitality in spite of the population loss and may actually experience increases in real per capita income as population declines. Other cities are experiencing rapid job loss without corresponding reductions in population and labor force, a combination that creates both high unemployment and losses in real per capita income. *Clearly, the healthy economic development of a city is*

2. William Alonso, "The Current Halt in the Metropolitan Phenomenon" (Paper prepared for Symposium on Challenges and Opportunities in the Mature Metropolis, Saint Louis, Missouri, June 6-8, 1977), p.12.

not so much a function of the level *of population or employment as it is
of retaining a reasonable* balance *between the two.*

Other problems are created by the changing characteristics of population and the employment base. The employment base includes many
activities other than manufacturing (the traditional base of economic
development); among these are exportable services (such as banking and
insurance), educational institutions, and a variety of nonprofit organizations. Therefore, although regional shifts and metropolitan decentralization are important in assessing the prospects of individual cities, they are
not the only factors that need to be considered.

Furthermore, not all important trends are so easy to measure as
those concerning population and business location. Nor will recent
trends affect all places in the same way. Therefore, predictions about
particular places based on these trends must be made with considerable
caution. Changes in federal policy or other outside forces could
significantly affect the future trends. Determined leadership and active
participation on the part of state and local governments, the business
community, and citizen groups could all affect their future course. In
cases where adverse trends cannot be halted or reversed, well-
coordinated public and private policies can do much to ameliorate the
problems and facilitate necessary adjustments.

Changes in Federal Policy

The federal government has a profound influence on the distribution
of population and economic activity. Research indicates that current
federal policy has reinforced the movement to the West and South and
the trend toward urban decentralization.

Many of the most important location consequences of federal activity stem from policies that do not have overt relocation objectives.[3] Both
these policies and policies targeted to specific areas need to be carefully
examined (and their results monitored) in order to develop a more complete picture of the federal government's potential for influencing trends
in population and economic location. For example, a recent Urban Institute study has shown that federal tax provisions historically have favored
low-density urban sprawl over compact development and have speeded
up the rate of decentralization in metropolitan regions. They have also

---

3. Tables 4 and 5 of the Appendix are from Roger J. Vaughan's work at the Rand Corporation on the federal
impact on economic development. They show his conclusions about the general interregional, intraregional,
and urban effects of a variety of federal policies.

favored investment in housing and other structures over alternative investments in the economy; construction of single-family, owner-occupied housing over multifamily, rental apartments; and development of new commercial, industrial, residential, and public buildings over maintenance and repair of older capital structures.[4] Therefore, even federal policies that have other objectives should be examined for their influence on the location of population and economic activity. Closer attention to these indirect effects could lead to altered federal choices that would influence location in ways more conducive to overall urban economic health.

Self-Correcting and External Forces

Even if there are no major changes in federal policies, regional population shifts and metropolitan area decentralization will not necessarily continue at the same rates. Two kinds of forces may operate against these trends: self-correcting forces that derive from growth or decline of population or economic activity and external forces.

Population movement and economic activity are often responses to differences in the availability and price of jobs, housing, and services in various areas. However, the movement itself affects prices and availability in areas where change occurs. For example, in areas where population and employment are growing, the demand for public services and private goods tends to increase, and wages tend to escalate. Moreover, if supply is not able to meet the demand, prices will rise. Both supply shortages and increased prices discourage further growth. Other forces may dampen decline; these include reduced demand for housing, increases in the availability of land, reductions in congestion, and selective reductions in the demand for some public services (such as those resulting from a decrease in the school-age population).

Many other important changes in the relative advantage of different places arise from forces other than those generated by population growth or decline. Federal policy is, as we have noted, an extremely important factor. So may be higher energy costs, availability of energy, availability of water, and the changing composition of households. High energy costs and concern about the availability of energy favor locations that are close to supplies or that reduce usage requirements. Availability of an assured water supply is a more recent factor that may have regional implications. Consequently, center cities may experience some transpor-

---

4. A summary of these effects appears in *Search: A Report from the Urban Institute* 7, no. 1 (Spring 1977). The full study will be published in 1978.

tation and fuel-efficiency advantages over suburbs. However, unless new energy sources are developed, these factors may also accelerate the regional shifts toward the South and Southwest. Within the last decade, new households have been forming at a much more rapid rate than the population has increased. There have been substantial increases in the number of households composed of one person, unrelated individuals, and married couples without children. These changes will affect the relative demand for various types of housing, and larger, more cosmopolitan cities may be favored by such nontraditional households.

But current regional shifts and decentralization trends are strong, and it is clearly too soon to declare that any of these factors will stop or reverse them. Nevertheless, it would just as clearly be shortsighted to ignore the forces working in the opposite direction.

Government, Business, and Citizen Leadership

It is difficult to measure the ability of people to learn both how to cope with change and how to create desired changes. Urban problems have not gone unnoticed by the leadership in state and local governments, business, and citizen groups. In many urban areas, there is an increased willingness on the part of these people to wrestle with the problems in constructive ways.

Most important, there is a growing recognition by local government officials and local business leaders of the need to create a public-private partnership that can focus effectively on jobs, neighborhood housing, and commercial revitalization. The need to provide jobs and earned income at the local level is widely recognized as the keystone of revitalization strategies for the cities, and local governments and business leaders are finding ways to cooperate in such efforts. (A forthcoming CED policy statement, *Jobs for the Hard-to-Employ: New Directions for a Public-Private Partnership*, will deal with this question in detail.) Business can participate in government-sponsored economic development planning groups. Business groups can plan, finance, and establish local development corporations through which both public and private interests can be channeled.[5] New initiatives are being taken to ensure

5. For a series of case studies on local development activities as they relate to integrated use of federal community development, economic development, and employment training programs, see National Council for Urban Economic Development, *Community, Economic and Manpower Development Linkages*, Sections 1 and 2, February 1976, Final Report to the U.S. Department of Housing and Urban Development, Office of Policy Research and Development, Contract H-2274.

local action to prevent further deterioration of the central cities, to redefine their functions if necessary, and to protect the economic base necessary for vitality. We recognize that not all cities will have the requisite desire or local leadership to develop and implement such initiatives. But for the cities that do possess these assets, there is promise of success. Therefore, it would be unfortunate if policy makers at the state and federal levels become so overwhelmed by the general trends that they fail to accept and support the plans of specific cities that have both the leadership and the will to undertake substantial revitalization efforts. The federal and state governments should also encourage further improvements in local capabilities.

The time is right to examine ways in which federal policies can be better targeted and tailored to aid cities that have critical problems and that also have local leadership dedicated to their resolution.

DIFFERENT CITIES, DIFFERENT PROBLEMS

Better use of federal policies tailored to solve the structural problems of the cities will depend to a considerable extent on clarifying the variety of problems among cities.

In some respects, all cities are unique; at the same time, groups of cities often have similar indicators of need. Partly as a result of differing population and industry shifts, local economies do not all make smooth adjustments to changes in the national economy. An indication of this is the wide variation in unemployment rates among local economies. For this reason, the local unemployment rate appears to be one useful indicator of some classes of problems. Change in population or employment in a city also creates problems that require significant adaptations on the part of both people and their governments. The severity of the problems and the degree of adaptation required can be expected to vary with the rate of change. For these reasons, unemployment and growth rates can provide a useful starting place for examining urban diversity. It should be emphasized at once that there are numerous dimensions of city life by which its sharp diversity could be defined. But unemployment and population growth rates are two of those dimensions that are easily measurable and represent very important developments in their own right. They are two distinctive, if not always unrelated, forces that are sometimes causes and sometimes consequences of other key city trends.

The Joint Economic Committee (JEC) of the U.S. Congress recently issued a study of the fiscal condition of a sizable sample of the nation's largest cities in which the cities were grouped into four classes according to population decline and growth and their unemployment rates:[6]

1. Cities with high unemployment rates (above the national average for 1976) and declining population (1970–1975)

2. Cities with low unemployment rates and declining population

3. Cities with high unemployment rates and growing population

4. Cities with low unemployment rates and growing population

Even this simple classification can be used to help sort out some of the great diversity of city conditions. Concrete examples are presented in the following paragraphs.

The cities in each of the above groups and their 1975 populations are shown in Figure 2 of the Appendix. In the sample, the declining cities are larger in size than the growing cities. The growing cities are predominantly in the South and West; there are none in the East and only two in the Midwest. The declining cities are mostly in the East and Midwest, but five are in the South and four in the West. Almost all the growing cities increased their center-city acreage substantially, primarily through annexation of adjacent territory in the 1960–1970 period; whereas only twelve of the forty-one declining cities increased their center-city acreage significantly during the same period.

In its report, the JEC argues that "maintenance and upgrading of the public infrastructure and particularly reversing the current downward trend in capital expenditures, appears to be the single greatest problem facing our nation's cities."[7] The report shows that capital expenditures have been significantly reduced. The capital budgets for the total sample decreased by 5 percent between 1976 and 1977. In high-unemployment cities, they decreased by as much as 13 percent. But whereas capital expenditures declined, the reported needs of the surveyed cities re-

6. U.S. Congress, Joint Economic Committee, *The Current Fiscal Condition of Cities: A Survey of 67 of the 75 Largest Cities* (Washington, D.C.: U.S. Government Printing Office, 1977).

7. U.S. Congress, Joint Economic Committee, *The Current Fiscal Condition of Cities: A Survey of 67 of the 75 Largest Cities*, p. 4.

mained extensive. The fifty cities that reported their capital needs to the JEC estimated a current capital need of $22.4 billion.[8]

Although all the cities in the sample had some fiscal difficulties, those with both high unemployment and declining population tended to be worst off.

- These cities have increased their total service expenditures by 3 percent during 1976. When the data are corrected for inflation, this actually represents a 3 percent *decline*.

- In spite of reducing capital budgets and real reductions in service expenditures, these cities substantially increased their taxes.

The cities in the sample with both high unemployment and declining population are in large metropolitan areas with high density and population clustering. Over 50 percent had an above-average concentration of jobs. In contrast, almost all the cities with low unemployment and growing population were in areas with low density and population spreading. Low density and a spread population are also found in many of the declining cities with low unemployment. Jobs tend, however, to be centralized in these cities. In the sample cities, low density and less concentrated population are more closely associated with lower unemployment rates than is the degree of job concentration in the center city.

Comparing this sample with the results of another study shows that growing cities tend to have less pronounced intra-area and intercity hardship than declining cities.[9] Once again, the sharpest differences are found between cities with both high unemployment and declining population and cities with both low unemployment and growing population. The high-unemployment, declining-population group contains the largest number of cities that are worse off than their suburbs and other central cities. The reverse is true of cities in the low-unemployment,

8. U.S. Congress, Joint Economic Committee, *The Current Fiscal Condition of Cities: A Survey of 67 of the 75 Largest Cities*, p. 2.

9. Richard P. Nathan and Charles Adams, *Understanding Central City Hardship*, Technical Series Reprint T-102 (Washington, D.C.: The Brookings Institution, 1976). The variables, which were used with equal weight in these indexes, were (1) unemployment (percent of civilian labor force unemployment), (2) dependency (persons under eighteen or over sixty-four years of age as a percent of total population), (3) education (percent of persons twenty-five years of age or over with less than a twelfth grade education), (4) income level (per capita income), (5) crowded housing (percent of occupied housing units with more than one person per room), and (6) poverty (percent of families below 125 percent of low-income level). The intrametropolitan index measured the relative hardship in the central city and its suburbs. The intercity index measured relative hardship of one central city relative to other central cities.

Figure 1

COMPARISONS OF INCOME, BY SOURCE OF INCOME, FOR CITY GROUPS, 1969 TO 1974

City Group	Labor and Proprietor Income			Transfer Payments		
	Percent Increase, 1969–1974	Percent of 1974 Income	Percent of Total Income Change, 1969–1974	Percent Increase, 1969–1974	Percent of 1974 Income	Percent of Total Income Change, 1969–1974
High unemployment rates and declining population	35.6	71.6	61.2	102.8	13.3	22.9
Low unemployment rates and declining population	41.7	75.3	66.7	114.3	10.7	17.9
High unemployment rates and growing population	56.9	74.1	67.8	129.4	12.3	18.0
Low unemployment rates and growing population	64.0	74.6	69.9	130.0	11.3	15.8

Source: Calculations by the Urban Institute from U.S. Department of Commerce, Bureau of Economic Analysis, *Local Area Personal Income, 1969–1974*, vols. 2–4 (Washington, D.C.: U.S. Government Printing Office, June 1976).

growing-population group. The growing cities achieved more growth in per capita income than the declining cities despite an expanding population base. On average, these cities also have higher per capita incomes than their suburbs (see Appendix, Figure 6, for the supporting data). This was largely a result of their ability to annex prosperous portions of adjacent territory during the 1960s.

Figure 1 compares the sample cities with respect to income from earnings (labor and proprietor income) and transfer payments.[10] Once

10. These data are not available by city. They are central-county data and should be interpreted with some caution because the central-city portion of the central county varies considerably.

again, those cities with high unemployment and declining population fared the worst. They are in counties that experience an average increase of income from earnings that was only a little over half the increase in the counties containing low unemployment and growing population. Transfer income represented a larger proportion of their recent income change than was true of the cities with low unemployment and growing population.

These income differences arise from high unemployment, the loss of high-wage manufacturing employment, and the relatively slow growth of employment in other sectors in these cities. Figure 2 shows changes in manufacturing, employment, and retail sales.

Although nationwide growth of manufacturing employment has been slow, the growing cities have captured more of it than the cities declining in population. Furthermore, manufacturing employment in the growing cities shows relatively balanced growth within both the central-city areas and the surrounding areas. Cities with both high unemployment and declining population have lost manufacturing employment at their centers and have the slowest growth of such employment in their suburbs. Retail sales present a similar picture. From 1963 to 1972, increases in retail sales in low-unemployment, growing cities were almost three times as high as in high-unemployment, declining cities. A modest increase in retail sales in the central business district in cities with high unemployment and declining population was dwarfed by the growth of retail sales in their suburbs. For the other city groups, the decline in retail sales in the central business district reflects a less centralized population and annexation of additional shopping centers away from the central area.

It should be noted that annexation of adjacent territory by the central jurisdiction is an important feature of the growing cities. This fact suggests that there should be continued efforts to ameliorate the structural problems of local government. Federal incentives may be needed to facilitate such efforts, but the states must bear the central responsibility because they alone have the legal authority to affect municipal powers and activities.

The preceding paragraphs amply demonstrate that there are important differences among the groups of cities classified by unemployment rates and population decline or growth. Furthermore, the cities with population declines tend to be worse off than the growing cities, whether both are experiencing high or low unemployment rates. The cities that tend to be worst off are those experiencing both decline in population

Figure 2

INTRAMETROPOLITAN COMPARISONS OF MANUFACTURING EMPLOYMENT AND RETAIL SALES FOR CITY GROUPS

City Group	Manufacturing Employment, 1972, as Percent of 1963		Percent Change in Central-City Retail Sales between 1963 and 1972	Percent Change in Retail Sales in Central Business District between 1963 and 1972	Percent Change in Retail Sales Outside Central City between 1963 and 1972
	Inside Central-City Areas	Outside Central-City Areas			
High unemployment rates and declining population	87.1	127.0	42.7	7.8	152.8
Low unemployment rates and declining population	107.9	152.1	66.1	-5.0	170.4
High unemployment rates and growing population	139.7	138.6	107.2	-4.1	137.2
Low unemployment rates and growing population	159.0	158.9	121.9	-8.1	161.0

Source: Calculations by the Urban Institute from Advisory Commission on Intergovernmental Relations, *Trends in Metropolitan America*, Information Report M-108 (Washington, D.C., February 1977), Table 13, pp. 47–49, and Table 14, pp. 50–52.

and high unemployment at the same time. This is a result, in part, of the disproportionately large share of out-migrants who have better work experience and prospects than many of the remaining unemployed.

There remains, of course, very substantial diversity even among cities in the same category of employment and population changes. Other forces are strongly at work shaping city destinies, and they are not

always closely correlated with employment or population trends. Therefore, careful attention should be given to such elements as the city's
fiscal situation, the income of its residents, the quality of its services, the
productivity of its labor force, and the capacity of its leadership.

As a practical matter, however, cities with declining population and
high unemployment can serve as easily identified candidates for priority
analysis of their need for outside assistance. On the strength of such
analysis, federal assistance programs ought to be tailored and targeted to
mesh most effectively with local conditions. Even in cases where it is
not possible or practical to halt a city's decline, well-designed federal
policies might help to cushion it and ease necessary adjustments. Economic development initiatives that are undertaken in partnership with
local leadership and that attempt to achieve a better balance between
population and jobs should play a major role in these policies. Such
initiatives can do much to retain a quality labor force, attract investment,
increase the tax base, and reduce the size of the dependent population.

A CONSTRUCTIVE FEDERAL POLICY
FOR URBAN AREAS

There is every reason to suspect that critical features of the urban
system will continue to change, sometimes in response to the decisions
of individuals and firms to move or stay and sometimes in response to
key decisions that commit the government to specific courses of action.
Some areas now in severe distress will improve; some now moving
forward will experience difficulty. For these reasons, there can be no
once-and-for-all solution to the urban problem. **A constructive federal
policy for urban areas must be flexible enough to adjust to change
and firm enough to be relied on. Furthermore, it must offer a set of
programs to alleviate specific problems.**

Past Approaches to Urban Policy

Federal approaches to urban policy have gone through several
transformations without developing mechanisms or leadership focused
on the complexities of urban change, the development of priorities, and
the integration of the federal response. The four major approaches to

urban problems attempted during the last several decades have suffered as a result.

Function The first approach was to deal with problems by function. Improving housing and education and reducing crime were identified as principal urban concerns, and major efforts were launched to accomplish each goal. Although some progress can be cited, the limited achievement of this approach can now be seen as partly attributable to the failure to recognize or act on the relationship of these concerns to other important functions, such as transportation, health, job creation, vocational training, income maintenance, local economic vitality, and neighborhood integrity. Moreover, each functional area is made up of numerous components. For example, crime control involves police, courts, correctional institutions, criminal codes enacted by legislatures, economic levels, family structure, and so on. Each of these components, in turn, involves numerous actors. For example, police services involve federal, state, regional, county, and local agencies and programs. Consequently, crime turns out to be considerably less than satisfactory as an organizing concept. The same could be said for most of the other major functional areas.

Structure A second approach dealt with the structure of government through which urban problems are handled. During the 1960s, a great deal of attention was given to the need for metropolitan-wide government that would reduce the fragmentation of jurisdictions; encourage integrated, area-wide management; and recapture the suburban tax base. However, in all but a few areas, such proposals are unable to overcome formidable political opposition from those, ranging from suburbanites to inner-city blacks, who felt threatened by such amalgamations. More progress was made in the creation of planning capability, but the resulting raft of planning agencies and personnel often bogged down in analysis or otherwise remained detached from policy making and implementation.

Although metropolitan government may be difficult to achieve, the cities that have adopted some form of it or that have annexed adjacent territory have generally improved their situation. No one form of reorganization can meet all needs. Diversity must be acknowledged and dealt with. There are a variety of community-metropolitan-regional forms that can, with strong state support, be tailored to cope with the various economic, cultural, and political characteristics of different areas.

Therefore, continued interest in these questions at the federal level is encouraging. Where political reorganization is impossible, state and federal incentives to encourage sharing of tax revenues throughout the entire metropolitan area would be desirable.

Some attention was also given to improving the structural division of responsibilities at various levels of government. Rather than deal with the vast problem of crime, the emphasis was on improving the organization and ability of institutions responsible for some narrower aspect of criminal justice. For example, the federal Law Enforcement Assistance Administration was to be principally a funding agency. State criminal justice planning agencies were to coordinate statewide efforts (including the distribution of federal funds). Metropolitan-wide police authorities would assure comprehensiveness in city and suburban police operations. And individual police departments would improve their management effectiveness in order to increase their ability to handle the problems they confront each day.

Such approaches, however, tended to ignore the need to determine which level or agency actually could do the job rather than which one was theoretically best able to handle it. For example, some aspects of crime control call for direct federal action. The sale of illicit drugs involves complex national and international networks for producing and distributing narcotics. Organized crime operates in many local and state jurisdictions. Federal laws invariably affect local crime-control operations. The influx of illegal aliens requires control by federal immigration agencies. The amount of crime related to youth unemployment may be a consequence of federal economic policies as well as of local crime-control operations.

Fighting Poverty A third approach concentrated on the problems of low-income city residents who, in the judgment of some, have been both the principal source and the principal victims of urban problems. A variety of policies developed during the 1960s were aimed at raising income levels, providing specific services (especially housing, food stamps, and medical care), and fostering greater community organization and political strength among the poor. Poverty has been inextricably related to race in most cities, and civil rights legislation and affirmative action programs were seen as important parts of the solution to the plight of low-income people.

Although such programs clearly had some effect on raising incomes and increasing opportunities for the poor or disadvantaged, they nonetheless dealt with only part of the problem. The economic decline of the late 1960s and early 1970s demonstrated the relative frailty of public poverty-fighting programs in the context of the total economy. Even the elimination of serious deprivation (if achieved) could not solve a host of other city problems that may result from the congestion and disorderliness of an abundant but poorly organized society.

Revenue Sharing A fourth approach attempted to stabilize the faltering fiscal condition of city governments. Cities have a disproportionate share of those residents who require public social services; whereas suburbs have a disproportionate share of those best able to pay taxes. Therefore, cities have had to bear the heavy burden of maintaining city services that are also used by suburban commuters and are generally important to the health of the entire metropolitan area. Revenue sharing, initially conceived as a means of redistributing the so-called fiscal dividend that was supposed to accrue to the federal government as its revenues grew faster than expenditures (and that did not materialize as expected), was enacted during the Nixon Administration as a way of bolstering local governments while easing the withdrawal of direct federal intervention in city problems.* The special revenue or block grant programs were designed to consolidate categorical grants into functional areas and return revenue to local governments, which would be permitted wider discretion in their use. Numerous proposals for the federal government and the states to assume a larger role in functional areas, particularly health, education, and income maintenance, were similarly aimed at relieving the increasingly hard-pressed budgets of local governments.

This approach, too, has had its shortcomings. Financial relief has been small compared with the needs of city governments.*   A substantial part of the redistribution has benefited suburban jurisdictions. And the assumption of major functions by state and federal governments has yet to take place. All these facts reflect the diminishing political power wielded by the cities in state legislatures and Congress. Even substantial fiscal relief would not resolve the unequal distribution of income or a host of other major problems faced by the cities.

Key Elements of a Federal Approach

The present Administration has stated its desire to develop the mechanisms and sustain the leadership necessary to help deal with the

*See memoranda by ROBERT R. NATHAN, pages 35 and 36.

problems of the cities. This important undertaking is formidable in its complexity. As we have indicated, we recognize that there is no once-and-for-all solution to urban problems, nor can there be any. Nevertheless, we believe that key elements of an urban strategy can be established. We offer them in this introductory statement as a first step in helping to focus the federal government's effort to improve its response to urban problems.

Systematic monitoring of the effects of federal policies on the distribution of the labor force and economic activity is essential. It is clear that federal policies have a significant impact on the location of population and economic activity. Their net effect has been to reinforce both the movement of population and economic activity to the South and West and the decentralization of metropolitan activity. In many cases, this effect has been a consequence of federal policies adopted for other reasons. Indeed, such indirect effects may have been more significant in determining location than federal policies specifically directed to particular jurisdictions. Therefore, the minimum requirement for federal policy is greater awareness and close monitoring of its effects on the movement of population and economic activity. Such scrutiny has never been undertaken on a consistent basis. Consequently, redistribution of population and economic activity, even though substantial, has usually not been considered in policy choice. Better monitoring of indirect effects and anticipation of future effects of federal policy are necessary to the creation of federal sensitivity to local development issues. When the monitoring effort reveals unintended and harmful effects, it should prompt immediate consideration of appropriate remedial steps, either by Congress or by the Administration.

The federal government should assume responsibility for direct income transfers to the poor.* Recent proposals for federal welfare reform are generally consistent with CED's recommendations on this subject. In particular, the proposals link income transfers with incentives to work, as recommended by CED in the 1970 policy statement *Improving the Public Welfare System.* However, this policy change will not have the desired effect on urban areas unless the federal government also takes steps to increase opportunities for private and public employment for those able to work. A forthcoming statement by this Committee, *Jobs for the Hard-to-Employ: New Directions for a Public-Private Partnership,* will recommend measures to achieve these objectives.

Federal policy must be sharply focused on economic development programs directly related to particular cities' problems and on

*See memoranda by FLETCHER L. BYROM, and by JOHN H. PERKINS, pages 34 and 35.

new mechanisms for ensuring effective federal participation. The central objectives of economic development are to increase per capita incomes and to ensure reasonable income-earning opportunities for all who are able to work. Achieving these objectives does not require that all cities experience population growth or that cities now declining in population return to their previous population peaks. What is needed is a set of incentives to achieve better mutual adjustments between population and employment opportunities. In some places, this may require the movement of people to locations that offer employment opportunities; in others, it may call for incentives for expanding job opportunities in places with a labor surplus.

Although we recognize the likelihood of a continuing need for public-sector employment to supplement private-sector jobs in the most distressed urban areas, we believe that there are increasing opportunities to develop private-sector jobs in many cities.* These opportunities arise from the cooperation of local government and business in identifying new development possibilities, determining risk and capital cost-sharing arrangements, and ensuring coordination of public and private investments. If sufficient federal assistance is provided for such integrated local economic development plans, more of these opportunities could be realized.

Because one set of strategies will not achieve economic development objectives in all places, the federal government must develop procedures for identifying priorities among places to be served and provide assistance for programs that best meet the needs of those particular places.

We recognize that federal budgetary resources are limited and that choices have to be made. These choices include selecting the places that are to receive priority attention (targeting) and determining the mix of programs that will be most effective in these places (tailoring).** Criteria for these choices need to be established. There are currently a wide variety of criteria for determining program eligibility and fund allocations for both categorical programs and block grants. Consequently, it is extremely difficult to ensure coherent and consistent federal participation in revitalization efforts at the local level.

Better and more equitable formulas for the distribution of federal aid, particularly revenue sharing, also need to be developed. At present, high-income suburbs receive revenue sharing and in some instances have even used these federal funds to reduce local taxes. Revenue sharing should be distributed on the basis of need, but it should also be

*See memorandum by R. MANNING BROWN, JR., page 36.

**See memorandum by JAMES Q. RIORDAN, page 36.

used to reward local tax efforts as measured by its relationship to average local per capita income. Similarly, a rational formula for the distribution of federal mass transit funds should be developed on the basis of need rather than the imaginative nature of the proposals. Allocation of federal funds for other programs should also be on the basis of need and should be designed to stimulate and reward maximum local effort and encourage local initiative and innovation.

We believe that improving the situation requires additional efforts to develop information about how cities and their problems vary and about the degree to which groups of cities have similar problems and can be expected to respond similarly to particular programs. The rate of population and economic decline or growth may provide a usable initial criterion for establishing priorities for special attention. Particularly in periods of rapid urban change, it is likely that local efforts will need to be supplemented by special federal assistance. **The federal government should encourage—at the very least it should not frustrate—both active efforts and developing potential of local leadership to bring together public and private resources for the productive resolution of the problems of the cities.**

A comparison of those cities with sharply differing characteristics provides clues for improved tailoring of public action. For example, cities that are afflicted with both high unemployment and declining population require a combination of welfare payments for the dependent population, renewed economic development efforts to increase jobs and income or relocation information and assistance for those unable to find jobs, and fiscal relief for their central-city governments. Welfare payments are required because the extensive migration of unskilled workers to urban areas had increased the dependent population and accelerated the demand for public services. Economic development and public employment efforts are required in such cities because of a relatively concentrated population near the central business district and because the city has lost a good deal of its traditional manufacturing employment and other private jobs. Federal subsidies will be required in many cases to overcome the adverse effect of investment risk in these cities. If, even with federal assistance, sound local plans for revitalization are not developed, relocation information and assistance will also be required. Fiscal relief is required because of an eroded tax base and the legal and political infeasibility of annexation. Moreover, because of the regional difficulties of the areas of which these cities are a part, metropolitan government, even if politically feasible, may not be an ideal option. This should not be interpreted as an indictment of metropolitan government. Rather, it implies the need for state and federal participation and incentives if significant tax sharing is to be achieved within metropolitan areas. Fiscal relief may also be required for those cities that are postponing needed capital maintenance and improvements as a result of their attempts to balance their budgets. Such suggested public policy initiatives might not stop decline in these cities, but they should slow its pace and facilitate needed adjustments.

Although they are experiencing fewer difficulties overall, cities with low unemployment and growing population may need different forms of federal attention. Because they are likely to have smaller proportions of dependent populations, they are less in need of increases in transfer payments. Because they are gaining both population and private capital, demands on public services in these cities are in many cases increasing faster than local public revenues can be expected to meet in the short run. In order to avoid short-term supply shortages, such cities could make use of a federal loan strategy (similar to that considered for some growth-inducing defense programs) that would provide front-end capital for needed public investments.

Developing improved criteria for targeting assistance and tailoring programs to local circumstances is important, but this effort needs to be supplemented by improved procedures for linking locally developed initiatives to needed federal participation. Many of the best examples of public-private partnership at the local level involve detailed negotiations between local governments and private industry that clearly identify the operational roles of each in revitalization efforts. There is no equivalent comprehensive link between the local area and the state or federal governments at this time. We believe that the federal government should attempt to establish such a link.*

We believe that the time has come for federal policy to recognize the diversity of local areas, to be prepared to respond to local needs, and to make use of all that can be learned at the local level about how improvements can be made. The federal government needs an approach that is both more flexible than categorical grants and more focused on specific plans than general revenue sharing. It must make a commitment to well-planned improvements in the nation's central cities.

*See memorandum by ROBERT R. DOCKSON, page 37.

32

QUESTIONS FOR FURTHER STUDY

CED's Subcommittee on Revitalizing America's Cities intends to follow this introductory statement with an intensive study of a broad range of urban problems and their potential remedies. A major part of that study is expected to concentrate on what local government, business, and community groups can do, rather than on the federal policy considerations discussed here. CED believes that these groups have vital roles to play in developing successful urban strategies. We realize that many questions about what can and should be done to improve America's cities and the lives of the people in them remain to be answered. In coming months, the Subcommittee will seek more definitive answers to questions such as the following:

What kinds of mechanisms have been developed at the local level to facilitate public-private cooperation in revitalization? Which have been most successful? Which have been unsuccessful? What are the most important criteria for judging success?

What kind of data are needed to provide better information about current demographic and employment trends? What other information is needed to develop projections of future conditions that might alter these trends?

How will changes in energy prices and availability affect where people will live and where businesses will locate?

How will changes in the rate of household formation and in the composition of households affect where people will choose to live? Can more be done to enhance the viability of neighborhoods?

How do the fiscal structure and fiscal situation of a local government affect revitalization efforts? How can required maintenance and upgrading of public infrastructure be accomplished in the face of fiscal strain? How effective would changes in local property tax practices (such as uniform statewide assessments and differential taxes on land and improvements) be in revitalizing cities?

How can cities prevent the loss of existing firms? How can employment in existing firms be increased?

What role should the states play in encouraging restructuring of local governments and in redistributing income through tax sharing?

What is the magnitude of the impact of federal policies on the location of population and economic activity? What are the disincentives to revitalization resulting from federal policy?

What would be required to facilitate better targeting and tailoring of state and federal programs to the specific problems of different local areas?

What can be done to increase the capability of local organizations to participate actively in economic development planning and upgrade local development plans?

When should the major federal and state programs be directed toward increasing job opportunities in cities? When should they be directed toward facilitating relocation of people to cities experiencing job growth?

Because deciding what to do is only part of the problem, what can be done to improve management and implementation of government programs addressed to urban problems? How can better coordination among government agencies best be achieved? What kinds of performance measures and incentives would be most effective in this regard?

Our continued study in this field is intended to help develop private and public programs for a better urban tomorrow.

Memoranda of Comment, Reservation, or Dissent

Page 9, by JOHN D. GRAY (Hart Schaffner & Marx), *with which* A. ROBERT ABBOUD, CHARLES KELLER, JR. *and* C. WREDE PETERSMEYER *have asked to be associated*

Although I note that this policy statement is the first in a series and focuses predominantly on federal efforts, I think it is essential that we understand from the very beginning that governmental actions will not suffice. Any solution to urban problems must be spearheaded by the private sector and have the support of local and state governments. Business and industry must take an active and continuing leadership role in revitalizing our cities, ameliorating the unemployment situation and the housing crisis for low income families. The mechanisms for solving these serious problems are by and large in the private sector. I would hope that future statements in this series will focus on these mechanisms — and the assistance of local and state governments.

Page 9, by FRAZAR B. WILDE, *with which* C. WREDE PETERSMEYER *has asked to be associated*

The paper entitled "An Approach to Federal Urban Policy" does not have my approval.

There is much good material in the policy statement, especially on the need for the federal government to assume a larger share of the national problems of the poor. On the other hand, the paper is wrong in asking the federal government to participate directly in the problems of individual cities. The relationship of cities under our form of government is primarily the responsibility of the states in which the cities are located. The paper recognizes the great diversity of problems of the different cities in the country.

Federal aid other than welfare, if it is justified, should be made to the states, and the states should determine how such aid should be distributed to the individual cities in their area. It is cumbersome, ineffective, and increases the delays and the judgment errors of a large bureaucracy if the federal government in Washington tries to determine the needs and solutions of the different cities in our country.

Pages 9 and 28, by FLETCHER L. BYROM, *with which* J. S. McSWINEY *and* ROBERT B. SEMPLE *have asked to be associated*

There is no question that the present welfare system needs restructuring. However, caution should be exercised in establishing any new welfare process that would concentrate funding in the federal government and rely principally on cash transfers tied to income levels. Transfer payments from government to individuals have soared in the past several years, reflecting in part response to a genuine need, and in part the temptation to increase the size of payments for political advantage. We must assure that a high degree of discipline is imposed on the determination of who benefits from direct cash grants so that the money goes only to those who genuinely need it and are entitled to it, and in order that the total magnitude of government transfers is appropriate to the growing fiscal constraints on government.

Pages 9 and 28, by JOHN H. PERKINS

I have reviewed the voting copy of "An Approach to Federal Urban Policy" and can be counted among those in general agreement with the statement.

In dealing with the urban poor, I feel that increased emphasis must be placed on developing the potential of individuals, with a goal of improving their self-sufficiency. The statement, "The federal government should assume responsibility for direct income transfers to the poor," is acceptable with the elaboration provided in the full text of this paper (page 28). In the summary version, however, it is so categorically stated that it is easily subject to misinterpretation. I feel it would be useful to expand this point to communicate our intent and spirit more clearly.

Page 27, by ROBERT R. NATHAN

The so-called "fiscal dividend" did materialize. But every time there was a need for fiscal stimulus in the economy, the adopted stimulus took the form largely of substantial cuts in income taxes. Each fiscal dividend can only be dispensed once.

The fiscal dividend anticipated as a result of the responsiveness of the federal progressive income tax became intermingled with the acceleration of tax revenues attributable to the inflationary impact on income distribution. Some of the tax cuts made repeatedly over the past dozen or so years have been designed to offset the inflationary impact on income taxes, but the tax cuts were also related to the so-called fiscal dividend.

Of course that dividend has not been as high as it would have been had the economy been functioning at higher rates of capacity utilization and lower rates of unemployment. One cannot expect to fight inflation with unemployment and slow growth and still achieve the fiscal dividend that would be associated with a more vigorous, expanding economy associated with more successful direct anti-inflationary and expansionist efforts.

36

Page 27, by ROBERT R. NATHAN

For a considerable number of years the fiscal and functional relationships between the federal government on the one hand and state and local governments — especially the urban areas — have lacked coherent and integrated policies. The mobilization of financial resources as between different levels of government and the division of responsibilities over functions and over management of these functions have not been rationally or clearly defined.

With respect to the revenue side of fiscal policy, the steady decline in federal tax rates has been paralleled by a steady increase in rates of state and local property and sales taxes. Federal income taxes are progressive and responsive to changing economic conditions. Sales and property taxes are far less progressive, if not regressive, and not highly responsive. The rise in the share of state and local revenues to total government revenues has tended to reduce the progressivity of the aggregate public financing system in the United States.

The federal government's increased financial participation in local activities, either through the assumption of functions or through revenue-sharing, should have given it clout in setting conditions or standards designed to counter the distortions associated with population movements whereby urban centers have more and more problems and less and less revenue to meet these problems, and suburban areas have more and more resources relative to the problems that have to be solved. Certainly if the federal government is going to assume more financial responsibilities for these difficult urban problems it should set conditions whereby the financial programs of state governments or the creation of metropolitan government financing mechanisms would counter the imbalance that has developed as a result of the rich and higher-income people moving to the suburbs and leaving worse problems within urban centers for the poor people to solve.

Page 29, by R. MANNING BROWN, JR., *with which* C. WREDE PETERSMEYER *has asked to be associated*

While this paragraph stresses the importance of developing the opportunities that exist for private-sector jobs, it also lends comfort to the view that the public sector should serve as employer of last resort. I question the wisdom of expanding the responsibilities of the federal government or any other level of government to provide supplemental employment over and above the genuine work needs of the public sector.

Page 29, by JAMES Q. RIORDAN

I approve the statement generally, but do not agree that federal aid can efficiently be targeted and tailored to individual local situations.

Page 31, by ROBERT R. DOCKSON, *with which* ROBERT B. SEMPLE *has asked to be associated*

The CED policy statement accurately portrays many of today's urban problems and provides some useful directions for their resolution. However, I find much in the report that is a restatement of the obvious. The text tends to be long on generalities and short on specifics. By enunciating widely accepted goals and objectives, the statement becomes a generalized set of truisms rather than a specific call for action. Who can disagree that "... the federal government must develop procedures for identifying priorities..." or that "The federal government should encourage the active and developing potential of local leadership to bring together public and private resources for the productive resolution of the problems of the cities."

The statement emphasizes that "federal policy must be sharply focused on economic development programs directly related to particular cities' problems and on new mechanisms for ensuring effective federal participation." This statement is obvious, but it is disappointing in that it does not provide specific suggestions and examples of the types of programs that this would entail. Although specific proposals are difficult to enunciate with respect to federal urban policy, CED has not demonstrated a leadership role by issuing this statement. In spite of the controversy that might result from specific proposals, this is the need — and the private sector of our economy is the loser by not having a meaningful statement from CED.

APPENDIX

Figure 1

CHANGES IN EMPLOYMENT IN SELECTED CENTRAL CITIES, BY MAJOR EMPLOYMENT SECTOR, 1958 to 1972
(thousands)

City	Major Employment Sector					Total Job Losses	Total Job Gains	Net Employment Shift	Total Employment, 1972 [a]	Net Shift as Percent of 1958 Employment
	Manufacturing	Retail Trade	Wholesale Trade	Selected Services	Local Government					
Chicago	−104.3	−32.0	−31.1	32.9	7.8	−167.4	40.7	−126.7	1,053.5	−12.0
Baltimore	−20.5	−16.1	−2.1	5.6	13.0	−38.7	18.6	−20.1	260.4	−7.7
Boston	−27.2	−14.6	−9.1	19.9	4.0	−50.9	23.9	−27.0	244.3	−11.1
Detroit	−24.0	−31.7	−12.1	0.6	0.6	−67.8	1.2	−66.6	421.5	−15.8
New York	−138.5	−31.4	−42.1	72.9	126.7	−212.0	199.6	−12.4	2,164.8	−0.6
Cleveland	−43.6	−20.5	−10.5	5.9	−1.0	−75.6	5.9	−69.7	319.0	−21.8
Pittsburgh	−2.3	−12.1	−9.7	6.0	−0.4	−24.5	6.0	−18.5	166.8	−11.1
Buffalo	−17.6	−10.3	−4.9	4.1	3.2	−32.8	7.3	−25.5	149.7	−17.0
Cincinnati	−8.1	−6.9	−1.0	31.3	5.4	−16.0	36.7	20.7	160.9	12.9
Jersey City	−9.6	−0.7	−0.6	1.5	−1.8	−12.7	1.5	−11.2	62.7	−17.9
Louisville	4.5	−1.5	0.6	4.0	0.4	−1.5	9.5	8.0	110.6	7.2
Milwaukee	−17.0	−5.6	−6.5	8.1	5.0	−29.1	13.1	−16.0	219.9	−7.3
Minneapolis	−0.5	−4.6	−4.8	9.2	0.4	−9.9	9.6	−0.3	148.3	−0.2
Saint Paul	9.4	−1.6	−0.8	5.5	−1.7	−4.1	14.9	10.8	86.8	12.4
New Orleans	−0.5	−3.9	−2.4	10.2	1.9	−6.8	12.1	5.3	115.5	4.6
Newark	−31.3	−12.1	−5.6	1.2	1.8	−49.0	3.0	−46.0	151.6	−30.3
Philadelphia	−84.0	−16.4	−13.8	16.3	6.0	−114.2	22.3	−91.9	541.4	−17.0
Rochester	−3.6	−4.0	−0.6	3.0	2.4	−8.2	5.4	−2.8	143.5	−2.0
Saint Louis	−38.6	−22.6	−11.1	5.1	1.1	−72.3	6.2	−66.1	273.3	−24.2
Washington, D.C.	−1.4	−9.1	−4.7	20.4	25.2	−15.2	45.6	30.4	158.6	19.2
Providence	−9.9	−5.8	−1.1	1.7	−0.4	−17.2	1.7	−15.5	80.6	−19.2
Kansas City	4.2	−0.4	−3.1	12.7	0.9	−3.5	17.8	14.3	140.1	10.2
San Francisco	−11.9	0.7	−11.6	21.5	5.4	−23.5	27.6	4.1	197.4	2.1
Oakland	−7.9	−4.5	−0.9	5.6	0.8	−13.3	6.4	−6.9	83.1	−8.3
Los Angeles	−7.3	22.7	−1.7	57.5	8.2	−9.0	88.4	79.4	625.3	12.7

[a] Sum of manufacturing, retail trade, wholesale trade, selected services, and local government employment, 1972.

Sources: U.S. Department of Commerce, Bureau of the Census, Census of Manufacturing, Census of Wholesale Trade, Census of Retail Trade, and Census of Selected Services for 1958 and 1972. Local government figures for 1958 from Census of Government, "Compendium of Public Employment," vol. 2, no. 2, and for 1972 from Census of Government, "Employment of Major Governments," vol. 3, no. 1.

Figure 2

CITIES, CLASSIFIED BY UNEMPLOYMENT RATE AND POPULATION CHANGE, WITH 1975 POPULATION

Group 1 Cities	Population	Group 2 Cities	Population	Group 3 Cities	Population	Group 4 Cities	Population
New York	7,481,613	Chicago	3,099,391	San Diego	773,996	Houston	1,326,809
Los Angeles	2,727,399	Dallas	812,797	Honolulu	705,381	San Antonio	773,248
Philadelphia	1,815,808	Indianapolis	714,878	San Jose	555,707	Phoenix	664,721
Detroit	1,335,085	Columbus	535,610	El Paso	385,691	Memphis	661,319
Baltimore	851,698	Kansas City	472,529	Miami	365,082	Jacksonville	535,030
Washington, D.C.	711,518	Minneapolis	378,112	Tampa	280,340	Omaha	371,455
Milwaukee	665,796	Oklahoma City	365,916	Sacramento	260,822	Tulsa	331,726
San Francisco	664,520	Fort Worth	358,364	Corpus Christi	214,838	Austin	301,147
Cleveland	638,793	Louisville	335,954			Tucson	296,457
Boston	636,725	Saint Paul	279,535			Baton Rouge	294,394
New Orleans	559,770	Birmingham	276,273			Saint Petersburg	234,389
Saint Louis	524,964	Wichita	264,901			Virginia Beach	213,954
Seattle	487,091	Richmond	232,652			Mobile	196,441
Denver	484,531	Dayton	205,986			Anaheim	193,616
Pittsburgh	458,651	Des Moines	194,168			Shreveport	185,711
Atlanta	436,057	Grand Rapids	187,946			Knoxville	183,383
Cincinnati	412,564					Fort Wayne	183,299
Toledo	367,650					Colorado Springs	179,584
Portland	356,732						
Long Beach	335,602						
Oakland	330,651						
Akron	251,747						
Jersey City	243,756						
Yonkers	192,509						
Syracuse	182,543						

Group 1. Cities with high unemployment rates (above the national average for 1976) and declining population (1970–1975).
Group 2. Cities with low unemployment rates and declining population.
Group 3. Cities with high unemployment rates and growing population.
Group 4. Cities with low unemployment rates and growing population.

Sources: U.S. Congress, Joint Economic Committee, The Current Fiscal Condition of Cities: A Survey of 67 of the 75 Largest Cities; and 1975 population figures from the Economic Development Administration, U.S. Department of Commerce, Washington, D.C.; and Deborah Norelli, of the Joint Economic Committee staff.

Figure 3

CHANGE IN POPULATION OF METROPOLITAN AND NONMETROPOLITAN AREAS, BY REGION, 1950–1960, 1960–1970, 1970–1974
(thousands)

	1950[a]	1960[a]	1970[a]	Percent Change, 1950–1960	Percent Change, 1960–1970	1970[b]	1974[b]	Percent Change, 1970–1974[c]
United States, total	151,326	179,323	203,300	+18.50	+13.37	199,819	207,949	+10.17
All Metropolitan Areas								
Total	94,579	119,595	139,419	+26.45	+16.58	137,058	142,043	+9.09
In central cities	53,696	59,947	63,797	+11.64	+6.42	62,876	61,650	−4.87
Outside central cities	40,883	59,648	75,622	+45.90	+26.78	74,182	80,394	+20.93
Metropolitan areas of 1 million or more in 1970	54,524	69,070	80,657	+26.68	+16.78	79,498	81,059	+4.91
In central cities	32,272	34,010	34,824	+5.39	+2.39	34,332	33,012	−9.61
Outside central cities	22,252	35,060	45,833	+57.56	+30.73	45,166	48,047	+15.95
Metropolitan areas of less than 1 million in 1970	40,055	50,525	58,762	+26.14	+16.30	57,570	60,985	+14.83
In central cities	21,424	25,937	28,973	+21.07	+11.71	28,554	28,638	+0.74
Outside central cities	18,631	24,588	29,789	+31.97	+21.15	29,016	32,347	+28.70
Nonmetropolitan Areas								
Total	56,747	59,728	63,831	+5.25	+6.95	62,761	65,905	+12.52
In counties with no place of 2,500 or more	—	—	—	—	—	7,191	7,551	+12.52
In counties with a place of 2,500 to 24,999	—	—	—	—	—	39,725	41,982	+14.20
In counties with a place of 25,000 or more	—	—	—	—	—	15,845	16,372	+8.31
In counties designated metropolitan since 1970	—	—	—	—	—	8,373	9,243	+25.98

a Figures relate to areas as defined for 1970.
b Figures relate to areas as defined for 1974, including later adjustments for 1970.
c Rate per decade.

Figure 3 (continued)

41

	1950 [a]	1960 [a]	1970 [a]	Percent Change, 1950–1960	Percent Change, 1960–1970	1970 [b]	1974 [b]	Percent Change, 1970–1974 [c]
Northeast, total	39,478	44,678	49,061	+13.17	+9.81	48,329	48,887	+2.89
All Metropolitan Areas								
Total	31,687	35,878	39,007	+13.23	+8.72	38,675	38,742	+0.43
In central cities	18,017	17,498	17,167	–2.88	–1.89	17,044	16,250	–11.65
Outside central cities	13,670	18,380	21,840	+34.46	+18.82	21,631	22,493	+9.96
Metropolitan areas of 1 million or more in 1970	21,289	24,222	26,109	+13.78	+7.79	22,776	25,494	+29.83
In central cities	12,723	12,304	12,132	–3.29	–1.40	11,985	11,272	–14.87
Outside central cities	8,566	11,918	13,977	+39.13	+17.28	13,791	14,222	+7.81
Metropolitan areas of less than 1 million in 1970	10,398	11,656	12,898	+12.10	+10.66	12,899	13,247	+6.74
In central cities	5,294	5,194	5,035	–1.89	–3.06	5,059	4,977	–4.05
Outside central cities	5,104	6,462	7,863	+26.61	+21.68	7,840	8,271	+13.74
Nonmetropolitan Areas								
Total	7,791	8,800	10,054	+12.95	+14.25	9,655	10,145	+12.69
In counties with no place of 2,500 or more	—	—	—	—	—	204	139	–79.66
In counties with a place of 2,500 to 24,999	—	—	—	—	—	5,146	6,118	+47.22
In counties with a place of 25,000 or more	—	—	—	—	—	4,305	3,888	–24.22
In counties designated metropolitan since 1970	—	—	—	—	—	2,413	2,190	–23.10

a Figures relate to areas as defined for 1970.
b Figures relate to areas as defined for 1974, including later adjustments for 1970.
c Rate per decade.

Figure 3 (continued)

	1950[a]	1960[a]	1970[a]	Percent Change, 1950–1960	Percent Change, 1960–1970	1970[b]	1974[b]	Percent Change, 1970–1974[c]
North Central, total	44,461	51,619	56,591	+16.10	+9.63	55,793	56,522	+3.27
All Metropolitan Areas								
Total	27,090	33,536	37,867	+23.79	+12.91	37,173	37,562	+2.62
In central cities	16,269	17,036	17,184	+4.71	+0.87	16,861	15,941	−13.64
Outside central cities	10,821	16,500	20,083	+52.48	+25.35	20,312	21,621	+16.11
Metropolitan areas of 1 million or more in 1970	16,246	20,064	22,572	+23.50	+12.50	22,039	22,077	+0.43
In central cities	10,100	9,839	9,411	−2.58	−4.35	9,282	8,622	−17.78
Outside central cities	6,146	10,225	13,161	+66.37	+28.71	12,757	13,455	+13.68
Metropolitan areas of less than 1 million in 1970	10,844	13,472	15,295	+24.23	+13.53	15,134	15,486	+5.81
In central cities	6,169	7,197	7,773	+16.66	+8.00	7,579	7,319	−8.58
Outside central cities	4,675	6,275	7,522	+34.22	+19.87	7,555	8,167	+20.25
Nonmetropolitan areas								
Total	17,371	18,083	18,724	+4.10	+3.54	18,620	18,960	+4.56
In counties with no place of 2,500 or more	—	—	—	—	—	2,219	2,197	−2.48
In counties with a place of 2,500 to 24,999	—	—	—	—	—	12,304	12,861	+11.32
In counties with a place of 25,000 or more	—	—	—	—	—	4,097	3,902	−11.90
In counties designated metropolitan since 1970	—	—	—	—	—	1,412	1,397	−2.66

a Figures relate to areas as defined for 1970.
b Figures relate to areas as defined for 1974, including later adjustments for 1970.
c Rate per decade.

Figure 3 (continued)

	1950 [a]	1960 [a]	1970 [a]	Percent Change, 1950–1960	Percent Change, 1960–1970	1970 [b]	1974 [b]	Percent Change, 1970–1974 [c]
South, total	47,197	54,973	62,812	+16.48	+14.26	61,603	65,703	+16.64
All Metropolitan Areas								
Total	21,410	28,853	35,173	+34.76	+21.90	34,416	37,046	+19.10
In central cities	12,162	15,619	17,890	+28.42	+14.54	17,609	17,592	−0.24
Outside central cities	9,248	13,234	17,283	+43.10	+30.60	16,807	19,454	+39.37
Metropolitan areas of 1 million or more in 1970	7,025	10,050	13,189	+43.06	+31.23	13,252	14,244	+18.71
In central cities	4,155	5,184	5,655	+24.77	+9.09	5,586	5,520	−2.95
Outside central cities	2,870	4,866	7,534	+69.55	+54.83	7,666	8,724	+34.50
Metropolitan areas of less than 1 million in 1970	14,385	18,803	21,984	+30.71	+16.92	21,164	22,803	+19.36
In central cities	8,007	10,435	12,235	+30.32	+17.25	12,023	12,072	+1.02
Outside central cities	6,378	8,368	9,749	+31.20	+16.50	9,141	10,731	+43.48
Nonmetropolitan Areas								
Total	25,787	26,120	27,639	+1.29	+5.82	27,187	28,657	+13.52
In counties with no place of 2,500 or more	—	—	—	—	—	4,027	4,494	+28.99
In counties with a place of 2,500 to 24,999	—	—	—	—	—	17,786	18,261	+6.68
In counties with a place of 25,000 or more	—	—	—	—	—	5,424	5,902	+22.03
In counties designated metropolitan since 1970	—	—	—	—	—	4,028	4,988	+59.58

a Figures relate to areas as defined for 1970.
b Figures relate to areas as defined for 1974, including later adjustments for 1970.
c Rate per decade.

Figure 3 (continued)

	1950[a]	1960[a]	1970[a]	Percent Change, 1950–1960	Percent Change, 1960–1970	1970[b]	1974[b]	Percent Change, 1970–1974[c]
West, total	20,190	28,053	34,836	+38.95	+24.18	34,094	36,837	+20.11
All Metropolitan Areas								
Total	14,391	21,328	27,373	+48.20	+28.34	26,795	28,693	+17.71
In central cities	7,247	9,794	11,555	+35.15	+17.98	11,362	11,867	+11.11
Outside central cities	7,144	11,534	15,818	+61.45	+37.14	15,433	16,826	+22.57
Metropolitan areas of 1 million or more in 1970	9,964	14,735	18,786	+47.88	+27.49	18,421	19,245	+11.18
In central cities	5,294	6,684	7,626	+26.26	+14.09	7,469	7,598	+4.32
Outside central cities	4,670	8,051	11,160	+72.40	+38.62	10,952	11,647	+15.86
Metropolitan areas of less than 1 million in 1970	4,427	6,593	8,587	+48.93	+30.24	8,374	9,448	+32.06
In central cities	1,953	3,110	3,929	+59.24	+26.33	3,893	4,269	+24.15
Outside central cities	2,474	3,483	4,658	+40.78	+33.74	4,481	5,179	+38.94
Nonmetropolitan Areas								
Total	5,799	6,725	7,463	+15.97	+10.97	7,299	8,144	+28.94
In counties with no place of 2,500 or more	—	—	—	—	—	741	722	−6.41
In counties with a place of 2,500 to 24,999	—	—	—	—	—	4,539	4,742	+11.18
In counties with a place of 25,000 or more	—	—	—	—	—	2,019	2,680	+81.85
In counties designated metropolitan since 1970	—	—	—	—	—	520	668	+71.15

a Figures relate to areas as defined for 1970.
b Figures relate to areas as defined for 1974, including later adjustments for 1970.
c Rate per decade.

Sources: U.S. Department of Commerce, Bureau of the Census, *Current Population Reports*, "Estimates of Population of [state name]: Counties and Metropolitan Areas," Series P-26, nos. 75-1 to 75-50 (Washington, D.C.: U.S. Government Printing Office, July 1974 and 1975); and *Censuses of Population* for 1950, 1960, and 1970.

Figure 4

URBAN EFFECTS OF FEDERAL POLICIES ON THE DEMAND FOR GOODS AND SERVICES

Federal Policy	Interregional Effects	Intraregional Effects	Effects on Type of Urban Area
Macroeconomic Policies			
Aggregate monetary and fiscal policies	Northeast conforms more closely to national cycles, grows more slowly, and responds more volatilely than other regions to aggregate national changes	Central cities appear to be more cyclically volatile than suburbs and suffer recessions more deeply	Urban areas with high employment concentration in durable goods industries experience volatile employment fluctuations. Large urban areas conform more closely than small ones to the national pattern. Large cities experience more rapid inflation than small ones
Automatic fiscal stabilizers	Unknown	Unknown	Unknown
Personal income tax changes	Favor high-income regions	Favor high-income suburbs	Unknown
Corporation income tax changes	Slight favor to growth regions	Unknown	Unknown
Investment tax credits	Favor growth regions	Favor growth suburbs	Unknown
Public works programs	Favor growth regions	Favor suburbs	Unknown
Public employment programs	Unknown	Favor central cities	Program grants have been concentrated in large cities
Federal Spending and Purchasing			
Aggregate tax and expenditure patterns	Favor low-income regions at the expense of the Northeast; tax receipts fall short of expenditures in growth regions	Expenditures are concentrated in central cities	Unknown
Defense contracts	New England and Pacific areas have benefited from high federal expenditures	Unknown	Unknown
Defense salaries	Concentrated in the South and West	Unknown	Unknown
Sewage and water treatment facilities	Unknown	Have aided suburban development	Unknown
Federal Transfer Payments	Have stimulated redistribution from rich to poor regions; Northeast receives higher per capita welfare payments than other regions. Retirement payments have benefited the Sun Belt	Unknown	Unknown

Source: Roger J. Vaughan, *The Urban Impacts of Federal Policies*, vol. 2, *Economic Development* (Santa Monica, Calif.: The Rand Corporation, June 1977). Summary Table S.1, p. x.

Figure 5

URBAN EFFECTS OF FEDERAL POLICIES ON PRICE
AND AVAILABILITY OF FACTORS OF PRODUCTION

Federal Policy	Interregional Effects	Intraregional Effects	Effects on Type of Urban Area
Labor			
Income redistribution and taxes	High unemployment and welfare payments in the Northeast may have led to a reduction in labor force participation and higher unemployment in that region	Unknown	Unknown
Minimum wage	Unknown	May have led to increased unemployment in central cities in which affected labor is concentrated	Unknown
Unionization	High membership rate in Northeast has resulted in higher wages that may have slowed growth	Unknown	Unknown
Occupational Safety and Health Administration	Affects regions according to industrial structure (results unknown)	Unknown	May affect older cities more severely
Manpower programs	Unknown	Tend to benefit central-city labor force	Unknown
Transportation			
Regulation	Increase in freight rates has encouraged decentralization Rail-based industries in Northeast have suffered with the rise of trucking	Rail-based central-city industries have suffered with the increase in trucking, which encourages suburbanization	Cross subsidy from large to small towns
Subsidies			
Highways	Have favored growth regions at the expense of Northeast Subsidy in construction from North to South and Mountain area	Favored suburbs	Favored poorer, smaller towns at the expense of larger towns
Waterways	Recent developments may have favored the South Have diverted trade-offs from rail	Unknown	Cities served by waterway systems have benefited at the expense of rail-based cities
Mass transit	Unknown	May encourage suburbanization of population	Smaller cities receive higher per rider subsidy
Rail	May favor Northeast in the future	May favor central cities	May favor large cities
Air	Unknown	Airports usually constructed in suburbs	Cross subsidy from large to small cities
Energy			
Regulation	Natural gas regulation has deprived the Northeast of gas supplies	Unknown	Unknown
Subsidies	Unknown	Unknown	Subsidies for rural electrification may encourage decentralization
Capital			
Tax structure	Unknown	Tax structure may have encouraged decentralization	Unknown
Regulation	Unknown	Pollution control may affect central cities more severely	Pollution control may affect older cities more severely
Subsidies, business loans	Unknown	May encourage central-city investment	Unknown

Source: Vaughan, *The Urban Impacts of Federal Policies*, vol. 2, *Economic Development*, Summary Table S.2, p. xi.

Figure 6

COMPARISONS OF PER CAPITA INCOME

City Group	1969–1974 Average Percent Change in Per Capita Income	Average Per Capita Income Ratio of Central Cities to Areas Outside Central City, 1973
High unemployment rates and declining population	43.1	0.89
Low unemployment rates and declining population	44.9	0.93
High unemployment rates and growing population	47.9	1.04
Low unemployment rates and growing population	50.1	1.04

Sources: Calculations by the Urban Institute from U.S. Department of Commerce, Bureau of the Census, "Population Estimates and Projections," *Current Population Reports*, Series P-25, no. 649-699, 1973 (revised) and 1975 population estimates and 1972 (revised) and 1974 per capita income estimates for counties, incorporated places, and selected minor civil divisions in (the 50 states) (Washington, D.C.: U.S. Government Printing Office, May 1977); and Advisory Commission on Intergovernmental Relations, *Trends in Metropolitan America*, Information Report M-108 (Washington, D.C., February 1977), Table 2, pp. 14–16.

Objectives of the Committee for Economic Development

For thirty-five years, the Committee for Economic Development has been a respected influence on the formation of business and public policy. CED is devoted to these two objectives:

To develop, through objective research and informed discussion, findings and recommendations for private and public policy which will contribute to preserving and strengthening our free society, achieving steady economic growth at high employment and reasonably stable prices, increasing productivity and living standards, providing greater and more equal opportunity for every citizen, and improving the quality of life for all.

To bring about increasing understanding by present and future leaders in business, government, and education and among concerned citizens of the importance of these objectives and the ways in which they can be achieved.

CED's work is supported strictly by private voluntary contributions from business and industry, foundations, and individuals. It is independent, nonprofit, nonpartisan, and nonpolitical.

The two hundred trustees, who generally are presidents or board chairmen of corporations and presidents of universities, are chosen for their individual capacities rather than as representatives of any particular interests. By working with scholars, they unite business judgment and experience with scholarship in analyzing the issues and developing recommendations to resolve the economic problems that constantly arise in a dynamic and democratic society.

Through this business-academic partnership, CED endeavors to develop policy statements and other research materials that commend themselves as guides to public and business policy; for use as texts in college economics and political science courses and in management training courses; for consideration and discussion by newspaper and magazine editors, columnists, and commentators; and for distribution abroad to promote better understanding of the American economic system.

CED believes that by enabling businessmen to demonstrate constructively their concern for the general welfare, it is helping business to earn and maintain the national and community respect essential to the successful functioning of the free enterprise capitalist system.

CED Board of Trustees

Chairman
WILLIAM H. FRANKLIN
Chairman of the Board (Retired),
Caterpillar Tractor Co.

Vice Chairmen
FLETCHER L. BYROM, Chairman
Koppers Company, Inc.

E. B. FITZGERALD, Chairman
Cutler-Hammer, Inc.

GILBERT E. JONES, Retired Vice Chairman
IBM Corporation

PHILIP M. KLUTZNICK
Klutznick Investments

RALPH LAZARUS, Chairman
Federated Department Stores, Inc.

ROCCO C. SICILIANO, Chairman
TICOR

Treasurer
CHARLES J. SCANLON, Vice President
General Motors Corporation

A. ROBERT ABBOUD, Chairman
The First National Bank of Chicago

RAY C. ADAM, Chairman and President
NL Industries, Inc.

E. SHERMAN ADAMS
New Preston, Connecticut

WILLIAM M. AGEE, Chairman and President
The Bendix Corporation

ROBERT O. ANDERSON, Chairman
Atlantic Richfield Company

WILLIAM S. ANDERSON, Chairman
NCR Corporation

ERNEST C. ARBUCKLE, Retired Chairman
Wells Fargo Bank

ROY L. ASH, Chairman
Addressograph-Multigraph Corporation

SANFORD S. ATWOOD
Lake Toxaway, North Carolina

THOMAS G. AYERS, Chairman and President
Commonwealth Edison Company

ROBERT H. B. BALDWIN, President
Morgan Stanley & Co. Incorporated

JOSEPH W. BARR
Washington, D.C.

ROSS BARZELAY, President
General Foods Corporation

HARRY HOOD BASSETT, Chairman
Southeast Banking Corporation

WILLIAM O. BEERS, Chairman
Kraft Corp.

GEORGE F. BENNETT, President
State Street Investment Corporation

JACK F. BENNETT, Senior Vice President
Exxon Corporation

JAMES F. BERE, Chairman
Borg-Warner Corporation

DAVID BERETTA, Chairman and President
Uniroyal, Inc.

HOWARD W. BLAUVELT, Chairman
Continental Oil Company

WILLIAM W. BOESCHENSTEIN, President
Owens-Corning Fiberglas Corporation

H. M. BOETTINGER, Director of Corporate Planning
American Telephone & Telegraph Company

DEREK C. BOK, President
Harvard University

JOHN F. BONNER, President
Pacific Gas and Electric Company

CHARLES P. BOWEN, JR., Hon. Chairman
Booz, Allen & Hamilton Inc.

ALFRED BRITTAIN III, Chairman
Bankers Trust Company

THEODORE F. BROPHY, Chairman
General Telephone & Electronics Corporation

R. MANNING BROWN, JR., Chairman
New York Life Insurance Co., Inc.

JOHN L. BURNS, President
John L. Burns and Company

FLETCHER L. BYROM, Chairman
Koppers Company, Inc.

ALEXANDER CALDER, JR., Chairman
Union Camp Corporation

ROBERT D. CAMPBELL, Chairman and President
Newsweek, Inc.

ROBERT J. CARLSON, Senior Vice President
Deere & Company

RAFAEL CARRION, JR., Chairman and President
Banco Popular de Puerto Rico

THOMAS S. CARROLL, President
Lever Brothers Company

EDWARD W. CARTER, Chairman
Carter Hawley Hale Stores, Inc.

FRANK T. CARY, Chairman
IBM Corporation

SAMUEL B. CASEY, JR., President
Pullman Incorporated

WILLIAM S. CASHEL, JR., Vice Chairman
American Telephone & Telegraph Company

JOHN B. CAVE, Senior Vice President,
  Finance and Administration
Schering-Plough Corporation

HUNG WO CHING, Chairman
Aloha Airlines, Inc.

*EMILIO G. COLLADO, President
Adela Investment Co., S.A.

ROBERT C. COSGROVE, Chairman
Green Giant Company

JOSEPH F. CULLMAN, 3rd, Chairman
Philip Morris Incorporated

W. D. DANCE, Vice Chairman
General Electric Company

JOHN H. DANIELS, Chairman
National City Bancorporation

RONALD R. DAVENPORT, Chairman
Sheridan Broadcasting Corporation

*DONALD K. DAVID
Osterville, Massachusetts

*Life Trustee

RALPH P. DAVIDSON, Publisher
Time Magazine

ARCHIE K. DAVIS
Chairman of the Board (Retired)
Wachovia Bank and Trust Company, N.A.

R. HAL DEAN, Chairman
Ralston Purina Company

WILLIAM N. DERAMUS III, Chairman
Kansas City Southern Industries, Inc.

JOHN DIEBOLD, Chairman
The Diebold Group, Inc.

ROBERT R. DOCKSON, Chairman
California Federal Savings and Loan Association

EDWIN D. DODD, Chairman
Owens-Illinois, Inc.

ALFRED W. EAMES, JR., Chairman
Del Monte Corporation

W. D. EBERLE, Special Partner
Robert A. Weaver, Jr. and Associates

WILLIAM S. EDGERLY
Chairman of the Board and President
State Street Bank and Trust Company

ROBERT F. ERBURU, President
The Times Mirror Company

WALTER A. FALLON, Chairman
Eastman Kodak Company

FRANCIS E. FERGUSON, President
Northwestern Mutual Life Insurance Company

JOHN T. FEY, Chairman
The Equitable Life Assurance Society of the United States

JOHN H. FILER, Chairman
Aetna Life and Casualty Company

WILLIAM S. FISHMAN, Chairman
ARA Services, Inc.

E. B. FITZGERALD, Chairman
Cutler-Hammer, Inc.

ROBERT T. FOOTE, Chairman and President
Universal Foods Corporation

CHARLES W. L. FOREMAN, Vice President
United Parcel Service

JOHN M. FOX, Chairman
H. P. Hood Inc.

DAVID L. FRANCIS, Chairman and President
Princess Coals, Inc.

WILLIAM H. FRANKLIN
Chairman of the Board (Retired)
Caterpillar Tractor Co.

DON C. FRISBEE, Chairman and President
Pacific Power & Light Company

CLIFTON C. GARVIN, JR., Chairman
Exxon Corporation

LELAND B. GEHRKE, Vice President, Finance
3M Company

RICHARD L. GELB, Chairman
Bristol-Myers Company

GWAIN H. GILLESPIE
Executive Vice President-Finance
Chrysler Corporation

HUGH M. GLOSTER, President
Morehouse College

LINCOLN GORDON, Senior Research Fellow
Resources for the Future, Inc.

THOMAS C. GRAHAM, President
Jones & Laughlin Steel Corporation

HARRY J. GRAY, Chairman and President
United Technologies Corporation

JOHN D. GRAY, Chairman
Hart Schaffner & Marx

JOHN D. GRAY, Chairman
Omark Industries, Inc.

WILLIAM C. GREENOUGH, Chairman
Teachers Insurance & Annuity Association

DAVID L. GROVE
Vice President and Chief Economist
IBM Corporation

TERRANCE HANOLD
Minneapolis, Minnesota

JOHN D. HARPER, Chairman, Executive Committee
Aluminum Company of America

SHEARON HARRIS, Chairman
Carolina Power & Light Company

FRED L. HARTLEY, Chairman and President
Union Oil Company of California

ROBERT S. HATFIELD, Chairman
Continental Group, Inc.

GABRIEL HAUGE, Chairman
Manufacturers Hanover Trust Company

H. J. HAYNES, Chairman of the Board
Standard Oil Company of California

H. J. HEINZ II, Chairman
H. J. Heinz Company

LAWRENCE HICKEY, Chairman
Stein Roe & Farnham

JAMES T. HILL, JR.
New York, New York

WAYNE M. HOFFMAN, President
Tiger International, Inc.

ROBERT C. HOLLAND, President
Committee for Economic Development

FREDERICK G. JAICKS, Chairman
Inland Steel Company

JOHN H. JOHNSON, President
Johnson Publishing Co., Inc.

SAMUEL C. JOHNSON, Chairman
S. C. Johnson & Son, Inc.

WILLIAM B. JOHNSON, Chairman
IC Industries

GILBERT E. JONES, Retired Vice Chairman
IBM Corporation

EDWARD R. KANE, President
E. I. du Pont de Nemours & Company

CHARLES KELLER, JR.
New Orleans, Louisiana

DONALD P. KELLY, President
Esmark, Inc.

JOHN C. KENEFICK, President
Union Pacific Railroad Company

JAMES R. KENNEDY
Essex Fells, New Jersey

TOM KILLEFER, Chairman and President
United States Trust Company of New York

PHILIP M. KLUTZNICK
Klutznick Investments

HARRY W. KNIGHT, Chairman
Hillsboro Associates, Inc.

WILLIAM F. LAPORTE, Chairman
American Home Products Corporation

RALPH LAZARUS, Chairman
Federated Department Stores, Inc.

RALPH F. LEACH, Chairman, Executive Committee
Morgan Guaranty Trust Company of New York

FLOYD W. LEWIS, President
Middle South Utilities, Inc.

FRANKLIN A. LINDSAY, Chairman
Itek Corporation

J. EDWARD LUNDY, Executive Vice President
Ford Motor Company

J. PAUL LYET, Chairman
Sperry Rand Corporation

RAY W. MACDONALD, Chairman
Burroughs Corporation

IAN MacGREGOR, Hon. Chairman and
    Chairman, Finance Committee
AMAX Inc.

DONALD S. MacNAUGHTON, Chairman
Prudential Insurance Co. of America

MALCOLM MacNAUGHTON, Chairman
Castle & Cooke, Inc.

G. BARRON MALLORY
Jacobs Persinger & Parker

ROBERT H. MALOTT, Chairman
FMC Corporation

AUGUSTINE R. MARUSI, Chairman
Borden Inc.

WILLIAM F. MAY, Chairman
American Can Company

JEAN MAYER, President
Tufts University

*THOMAS B. McCABE, Chairman, Finance Committee
Scott Paper Company

C. PETER McCOLOUGH, Chairman
Xerox Corporation

GEORGE C. McGHEE
Washington, D.C.

JAMES W. McKEE, JR., President
CPC International Inc.

CHARLES A. McLENDON, Executive Vice President
Burlington Industries, Inc.

CHAMPNEY A. McNAIR, Vice Chairman
Trust Company of Georgia

E. L. McNEELY, Chairman
The Wickes Corporation

RENE C. McPHERSON, Chairman
Dana Corporation

J. W. McSWINEY, Chairman
The Mead Corporation

CHAUNCEY J. MEDBERRY III, Chairman
Bank of America N.T. & S.A.

LOUIS W. MENK, Chairman
Burlington Northern, Inc.

RUBEN F. METTLER, Chairman
TRW, Inc.

CHARLES A. MEYER, Vice President and Director
Sears, Roebuck and Co.

ROBERT R. NATHAN, President
Robert R. Nathan Associates, Inc.

EDWARD N. NEY, Chairman
Young & Rubicam Inc.

WILLIAM S. OGDEN, Executive Vice President
The Chase Manhattan Bank

THOMAS O. PAINE, President
Northrop Corporation

EDWARD L. PALMER, Chairman, Executive Committee
Citibank, N.A.

RUSSELL E. PALMER, Managing Partner
Touche Ross & Co.

VICTOR H. PALMIERI, President
Victor Palmieri and Company Incorporated

DANIEL PARKER
Washington, D.C.

JOHN H. PERKINS, President
Continental Illinois National Bank
    and Trust Company of Chicago

HOWARD C. PETERSEN, Chairman
The Fidelity Bank

C. WREDE PETERSMEYER, Retired Chairman
Corinthian Broadcasting Corporation

MARTHA E. PETERSON, President
Beloit College

PETER G. PETERSON, Chairman
Lehman Brothers, Inc.

JOHN G. PHILLIPS, Chairman
The Louisiana Land and Exploration Company

THOMAS L. PHILLIPS, Chairman
Raytheon Company

CHARLES J. PILLIOD, JR., Chairman of the Board
The Goodyear Tire & Rubber Company

JOHN B. M. PLACE, Chairman and President
The Anaconda Company

DONALD C. PLATTEN, Chairman
Chemical Bank

EDMUND T. PRATT, JR., Chairman
Pfizer Inc.

R. STEWART RAUCH, JR., Chairman
The Philadelphia Saving Fund Society

JAMES Q. RIORDAN, Executive Vice President
Mobil Oil Corporation

MELVIN J. ROBERTS
Colorado National Bankshares, Inc.

AXEL G. ROSIN, Chairman
Book-of-the-Month Club, Inc.

WILLIAM M. ROTH
San Francisco, California

JOHN SAGAN, Vice President-Treasurer
Ford Motor Company

JOHN C. SAWHILL, President
New York University

CHARLES J. SCANLON, Vice President
General Motors Corporation

HENRY B. SCHACHT, Chairman
Cummins Engine Company, Inc.

ROBERT M. SCHAEBERLE, Chairman
Nabisco Inc.

JOHN A. SCHNEIDER, President
CBS Broadcast Group

*Life Trustee

J. L. SCOTT, Chairman
Great Atlantic & Pacific Tea Company

WILTON E. SCOTT, Chairman
Tenneco Inc.

D. C. SEARLE, Chairman, Executive Committee
G. D. Searle & Co.

RICHARD B. SELLARS, Chairman, Finance Committee
Johnson & Johnson

ROBERT V. SELLERS, Chairman
Cities Service Company

ROBERT B. SEMPLE, Chairman
BASF Wyandotte Corporation

MARK SHEPHERD, JR., Chairman
Texas Instruments Incorporated

RICHARD R. SHINN, President
Metropolitan Life Insurance Company

GEORGE P. SHULTZ, President
Bechtel Corporation

FORREST N. SHUMWAY, President
The Signal Companies, Inc.

ROCCO C. SICILIANO, Chairman
TICOR

ANDREW C. SIGLER, President
Champion International Corporation

GRANT G. SIMMONS, JR., Chairman
Simmons Company

WILLIAM P. SIMMONS, President
First National Bank & Trust Company

L. EDWIN SMART, Chairman
Trans World Airlines

DONALD B. SMILEY, Chairman
R. H. Macy & Co., Inc.

RICHARD M. SMITH, Vice Chairman
Bethlehem Steel Corporation

ROGER B. SMITH, Executive Vice President
General Motors Corporation

ELVIS J. STAHR, President
National Audubon Society

CHARLES B. STAUFFACHER, President
Field Enterprises, Inc.

EDGAR B. STERN, JR., President
Royal Street Corporation

J. PAUL STICHT, President
R. J. Reynolds Industries, Inc.

GEORGE A. STINSON, Chairman
National Steel Corporation

*WILLIAM C. STOLK
Weston, Connecticut

WILLIS A. STRAUSS, Chairman
Northern Natural Gas Company

WALTER N. THAYER, President
Whitney Communications Corporation

WAYNE E. THOMPSON, Senior Vice President
Dayton Hudson Corporation

CHARLES C. TILLINGHAST, JR.
New York, New York

HOWARD S. TURNER, Chairman
Turner Construction Company

L. S. TURNER, JR., Executive Vice President
Texas Utilities Company

J. W. VAN GORKOM, President
Trans Union Corporation

ALVIN W. VOGTLE, JR., President
The Southern Company, Inc.

SIDNEY J. WEINBERG, JR., Partner
Goldman, Sachs & Co.

WILLIAM H. WENDEL, President
The Carborundum Company

GEORGE L. WILCOX, Director-Officer
Westinghouse Electric Corporation

*FRAZAR B. WILDE, Chairman Emeritus
Connecticut General Life Insurance Company

J. KELLEY WILLIAMS, President
First Mississippi Corporation

JOHN H. WILLIAMS, Chairman
The Williams Companies

*W. WALTER WILLIAMS
Seattle, Washington

MARGARET S. WILSON, Chairman
Scarbroughs

RICHARD D. WOOD, Chairman and President
Eli Lilly and Company

*Life Trustee

Honorary Trustees

CARL E. ALLEN
North Muskegon, Michigan

JAMES L. ALLEN, Hon. Chairman
Booz, Allen & Hamilton, Inc.

FRANK ALTSCHUL
New York, New York

O. KELLEY ANDERSON
Chairman, Executive Committee
Real Estate Investment Trust of America

JERVIS J. BABB
Wilmette, Illinois

S. CLARK BEISE, President (Retired)
Bank of America N.T. & S.A.

HAROLD H. BENNETT
Salt Lake City, Utah

WALTER R. BIMSON, Chairman Emeritus
Valley National Bank

JOSEPH L. BLOCK, Former Chairman
Inland Steel Company

ROGER M. BLOUGH
Hawley, Pennsylvania

FRED J. BORCH
New Canaan, Connecticut

MARVIN BOWER, Director
McKinsey & Company, Inc.

THOMAS D. CABOT
Honorary Chairman of the Board
Cabot Corporation

EVERETT N. CASE
Van Hornesville, New York

WALKER L. CISLER
Overseas Advisory Service

JOHN L. COLLYER
Vero Beach, Florida

JAMES B. CONANT
New York, New York

STEWART S. CORT, Director
Bethlehem Steel Corporation

GARDNER COWLES, Hon. Chairman of the Board
Cowles Communications, Inc.

GEORGE S. CRAFT
Atlanta, Georgia

JOHN P. CUNNINGHAM, Hon. Chairman of the Board
Cunningham & Walsh, Inc.

DONALD C. DAYTON, Director
Dayton Hudson Corporation

DOUGLAS DILLON, Chairman, Executive Committee
Dillon, Read and Co. Inc.

ROBERT W. ELSASSER
New Orleans, Louisiana

EDMUND FITZGERALD
Milwaukee, Wisconsin

WILLIAM C. FOSTER
Washington, D.C.

CLARENCE FRANCIS
New York, New York

GAYLORD FREEMAN
Chicago, Illinois

PAUL S. GEROT, Hon. Chairman of the Board
The Pillsbury Company

CARL J. GILBERT
Dover, Massachusetts

KATHARINE GRAHAM, Chairman
The Washington Post Company

MICHAEL L. HAIDER
New York, New York

WALTER A. HAAS, JR., Chairman
Levi Strauss and Co.

J. V. HERD, Director
The Continental Insurance Companies

WILLIAM A. HEWITT, Chairman
Deere & Company

OVETA CULP HOBBY, Chairman
The Houston Post

GEORGE F. JAMES
Cos Cob, Connecticut

HENRY R. JOHNSTON
Ponte Vedra Beach, Florida

THOMAS ROY JONES
Consultant, Schlumberger Limited

FREDERICK R. KAPPEL
Sarasota, Florida

DAVID M. KENNEDY
Salt Lake City, Utah

CHARLES N. KIMBALL, Chairman
Midwest Research Institute

SIGURD S. LARMON
New York, New York

ROY E. LARSEN, Vice Chairman of the Board
Time Inc.

DAVID E. LILIENTHAL, Chairman
Development and Resources Corporation

ELMER L. LINDSETH
Shaker Heights, Ohio

JAMES A. LINEN, Consultant
Time Inc.

GEORGE H. LOVE, Hon. Chairman
Consolidation Coal Company, Inc.

ROBERT A. LOVETT, Partner
Brown Brothers Harriman & Co.

ROY G. LUCKS
Del Monte Corporation

FRANKLIN J. LUNDING, Director
Jewel Companies, Inc.

FRANK L. MAGEE
Stahlstown, Pennsylvania

STANLEY MARCUS, Consultant
Carter Hawley Hale Stores, Inc.

JOSEPH A. MARTINO, Hon. Chairman
N L Industries, Inc.

OSCAR G. MAYER, Retired Chairman
Oscar Mayer & Co.

L. F. McCOLLUM
Houston, Texas

JOHN A. McCONE
Los Angeles, California

JOHN F. MERRIAM
San Francisco, California

LORIMER D. MILTON
Citizens Trust Company

DON G. MITCHELL
Summit, New Jersey

MALCOLM MUIR
Former Chairman and Editor-in-Chief
Newsweek

ALFRED C. NEAL
Harrison, New York

J. WILSON NEWMAN
Chairman, Finance Committee
Dun & Bradstreet Companies, Inc.

AKSEL NIELSEN, Chairman, Finance Committee
Ladd Petroleum Corporation

JAMES F. OATES, JR.
Chicago, Illinois

W. A. PATTERSON, Hon. Chairman
United Air Lines

EDWIN W. PAULEY, Chairman
Pauley Petroleum, Inc.

MORRIS B. PENDLETON
Vernon, California

JOHN A. PERKINS
Berkeley, California

RUDOLPH A. PETERSON, President (Retired)
Bank of America N.T. & S.A.

DONALD C. POWER
Galloway, Ohio

PHILIP D. REED
New York, New York

RAYMOND RUBICAM
Scottsdale, Arizona

GEORGE RUSSELL
Bloomfield Hills, Michigan

E. C. SAMMONS
Chairman of the Board (Emeritus)
The United States National Bank of Oregon

ELLERY SEDGWICK, JR.
Chairman, Executive Committee
Medusa Corporation

LEON SHIMKIN, Chairman
Simon and Schuster, Inc.

NEIL D. SKINNER
Indianapolis, Indiana

ELLIS D. SLATER
Landrum, South Carolina

DONALD C. SLICHTER
Milwaukee, Wisconsin

S. ABBOT SMITH
Boston, Massachusetts

DAVIDSON SOMMERS, Vice Chairman
Overseas Development Council

PHILIP SPORN
New York, New York

ROBERT C. SPRAGUE, Hon. Chairman of the Board
Sprague Electric Company

ALLAN SPROUL
Kentfield, California

FRANK STANTON
New York, New York

SYDNEY STEIN, JR., Partner
Stein Roe & Farnham

ALEXANDER L. STOTT
Fairfield, Connecticut

ANNA LORD STRAUSS
New York, New York

FRANK L. SULZBERGER
Chicago, Illinois

CHARLES P. TAFT
Cincinnati, Ohio

C. A. TATUM, JR., Chairman
Texas Utilities Company

ALAN H. TEMPLE
New York, New York

LESLIE H. WARNER
Darien, Connecticut

ROBERT C. WEAVER
Department of Urban Affairs
Hunter College

JAMES E. WEBB
Washington, D.C.

J. HUBER WETENHALL
New York, New York

JOHN H. WHEELER, President
Mechanics and Farmers Bank

A. L. WILLIAMS, Chairman, Finance Committee
IBM Corporation

*WALTER W. WILSON
Rye, New York

ARTHUR M. WOOD, Chairman
Sears, Roebuck and Co.

THEODORE O. YNTEMA
Department of Economics
Oakland University

*CED Treasurer Emeritus

Trustees on Leave for Government Service

W. GRAHAM CLAYTOR, JR.
Secretary of the Navy

ALONZO L. McDONALD, JR.
Deputy Special Representative for Trade Negotiations

Research Advisory Board

Chairman
PETER O. STEINER
Professor of Economics and Law
The University of Michigan

PAUL W. McCRACKEN
Graduate School of Business Administration
The University of Michigan

ROBERT J. MOWITZ, Director
Institute of Public Administration
The Pennsylvania State University

ANTHONY G. OETTINGER, Director
Program on Information Technologies and Public Policy
Harvard University

MARLENE ROSE ADELMAN
Director of Counseling and Testing
Norwalk Community College

RICHARD L. GARWIN
Thomas J. Watson Research Center
IBM Corporation

CARL KAYSEN
School of Humanities & Social Sciences
Massachusetts Institute of Technology

THOMAS C. SCHELLING
Public Policy Program
John Fitzgerald Kennedy School of Government
Harvard University

LEONARD SILK
Economic Affairs Columnist
The New York Times

JAMES Q. WILSON
Department of Government
Harvard University

CED Professional and Administrative Staff

ROBERT C. HOLLAND
President

FRANK W. SCHIFF, *Vice President and Chief Economist*

SOL HURWITZ, *Vice President, Information/Administration*

S. CHARLES BLEICH, *Vice President, Finance, and Secretary, Board of Trustees*

ELIZABETH J. LUCIER, *Comptroller*

Government Studies
R. SCOTT FOSLER, *Director*

Economic Research
SEONG H. PARK, *Economist*

Information and Publications
CLAUDIA P. FEUREY, *Associate Director*
ROBERT F. CORYELL, *Associate Director*
MARY C. MUGIVAN, *Publications Coordinator*
HECTOR GUENTHER, *Staff Associate*

Business-Government Relations
KENNETH M. DUBERSTEIN, *Director,
and Secretary, Research and Policy Committee*
SHAWN BERNSTEIN, *Staff Associate*

Finance
PATRICIA M. O'CONNELL, *Associate Director*
HUGH D. STIER, JR., *Associate Director*

Conferences
RUTH MUNSON, *Manager*

Administrative Assistants to the President
THEODORA BOSKOVIC
SHIRLEY R. SHERMAN

Statements on National Policy
Issued by the Research and Policy Committee
(publications in print)

Jobs for the Hard-to-Employ: New Directions for a Public-Private Partnership *(January 1978)*

An Approach to Federal Urban Policy *(December 1977)*

Key Elements of a National Energy Strategy *(June 1977)*

The Economy in 1977-78: Strategy for an Enduring Expansion *(December 1976)*

Nuclear Energy and National Security *(September 1976)*

Fighting Inflation and Promoting Growth *(August 1976)*

Improving Productivity in State and Local Government *(March 1976)*

*International Economic Consequences of High-Priced Energy *(September 1975)*

Broadcasting and Cable Television: Policies for Diversity and Change *(April 1975)*

Achieving Energy Independence *(December 1974)*

A New U.S. Farm Policy for Changing World Food Needs *(October 1974)*

Congressional Decision Making for National Security *(September 1974)*

*Toward a New International Economic System:
A Joint Japanese-American View *(June 1974)*

More Effective Programs for a Cleaner Environment *(April 1974)*

The Management and Financing of Colleges *(October 1973)*

Strengthening the World Monetary System *(July 1973)*

Financing the Nation's Housing Needs *(April 1973)*

Building a National Health-Care System *(April 1973)*

*A New Trade Policy Toward Communist Countries *(September 1972)*

High Employment Without Inflation:
A Positive Program for Economic Stabilization *(July 1972)*

Reducing Crime and Assuring Justice *(June 1972)*

Military Manpower and National Security *(February 1972)*

The United States and the European Community *(November 1971)*

Improving Federal Program Performance *(September 1971)*

Social Responsibilities of Business Corporations *(June 1971)*

Education for the Urban Disadvantaged:
  From Preschool to Employment *(March 1971)*

Further Weapons Against Inflation *(November 1970)*

Making Congress More Effective *(September 1970)*

Training and Jobs for the Urban Poor *(July 1970)*

Improving the Public Welfare System *(April 1970)*

Reshaping Government in Metropolitan Areas *(February 1970)*

Economic Growth in the United States *(October 1969)*

Assisting Development in Low-Income Countries *(September 1969)*

*Nontariff Distortions of Trade *(September 1969)*

Fiscal and Monetary Policies for Steady Economic Growth *(January 1969)*

Financing a Better Election System *(December 1968)*

Innovation in Education: New Directions for the American School *(July 1968)*

Modernizing State Government *(July 1967)*

*Trade Policy Toward Low-Income Countries *(June 1967)*

How Low Income Countries Can Advance Their Own Growth *(September 1966)*

Modernizing Local Government *(July 1966)*

Budgeting for National Objectives *(January 1966)*

Educating Tomorrow's Managers *(October 1964)*

Improving Executive Management in the Federal Government *(July 1964)*

Economic Literacy for Americans *(March 1962)*

---

*Statements issued in association with CED counterpart organizations in
 foreign countries.*

CED Counterpart Organizations in Foreign Countries

Close relationships exist between the Committee for Economic Development and independent, nonpolitical research organizations in other countries. Such counterpart groups are composed of business executives and scholars and have objectives similar to those of CED, which they pursue by similarly objective methods. CED cooperates with these organizations on research and study projects of common interest to the various countries concerned. This program has resulted in a number of joint policy statements involving such international matters as East-West trade, assistance to the developing countries, and the reduction of nontariff barriers to trade.

CEDA	Committee for Economic Development of Australia *139 Macquarie Street, Sydney 2001,* *New South Wales, Australia*
CEPES	Europäische Vereinigung für Wirtschaftliche und Soziale Entwicklung *Reuterweg 14, 6000 Frankfurt/Main, West Germany*
IDEP	Institut de l'Entreprise *6, rue Clément-Marot, 75008 Paris, France*
経済同友会	Keizai Doyukai (Japan Committee for Economic Development) *Japan Industrial Club Bldg.* *1 Marunouchi, Chiyoda-ku, Tokyo, Japan*
PEP	Political and Economic Planning *12 Upper Belgrave Street, London, SWIX 8BB, England*
SNS	Studieförbundet Näringsliv och Samhälle *Sköldungagatan, 2, 11427 Stockholm, Sweden*